As Dawn Ends the Night

As Dawn Ends the Night

AKIVA TATZ

Targum Press

Copyright © 2018 by A. Tatz

All rights reserved

ISBN 978-1-61465-504-6
No part of this publication may be translated, reproduced, stored in a retrieval system, or transmitted in any form or by any means, electronic, mechanical, photocopying, recording, or otherwise, without prior permission in writing from both the copyright holder and the publisher.

Distributed by:
Menucha Publishers, Inc.
1235 38th Street
Brooklyn, NY 11218
Tel/Fax: 718-232-0856

www.menuchapublishers.com

sales@menuchapublishers.com

Distributed in Israel by:
Yehuda Dombey
Cell: 054-864-4422
ydombey@gmail.com

Printed in Israel

Dedicated to

Mr. Howard H. Triest
Chaim ben Baruch

1923 - 2016

Born in Germany, fled in 1939, returned as an American soldier and served as interpreter at the Nuremberg Trials at which those responsible for the deaths of millions - including his own parents at Auschwitz - were convicted

by

Jonathon and Jessica Triest

and the

Triest Family

Contents

Acknowledgments	9
Preface	11

THE FADING OF HISTORY
Light to Darkness	15
The Modern Mind - Miracles to Materialism	19
Decline of the Generations	21
Knesset HaGedolah - The Great Assembly	31

HISTORICAL TRANSITIONS
The Closing of Prophecy	41
From Idolatry to Atheism	49

THE ORAL LAW & THE POWER OF THE SAGES
The Oral Law	53
Not in Heaven	56
Later Generations Do Not Argue with Earlier Ones	59
The Sage is Greater than the Prophet	61
Ravens and Doves - Torah Forms Reality	63
On the Shoulders of Giants	65
The Origins of Argument	69
Mutually Exclusive Truths	73
The Sealing of the Talmud	75
The Sages and Scientific Error	77

NEW MODES OF BEING
Breakaways and Reforms	83
End of Miracles	87
Miracle within Miracle - Revealing the Name	89
What was Revealed at Sinai?	93
The Problem of Later Miracles	94
Blessings Composed	99
Prayers Composed	103
Change of Language	107
Language and the Tower of Babel	109
From Seeing to Hearing	115
The New Beauty	119

NEW FESTIVALS, NEW TORAH

Purim	131
As Dawn Ends the Night	132
Torah Received Twice	134
Free Will Under Duress, Repentance Under Pressure	135
Purim and the Problem of Doubt	140
The New Work of Faith	141
New World, New Conduct	142
From Rebuke to Flattery	145
Israel and Greece	149
Science and Miracles	151
What are Laws of Nature?	153
A Conditional Creation	154
Sanctity of Joshua, Sanctity of Ezra	160
Chanuka	163
Healing of the Legs	165
A Prophet May Not Add	169
Tisha B'Av - Why Mourning Lessens	173

PERSONALITIES OF TRANSITION

Three Fathers who Began History - Twice	181
Transitional Personalities - Daniel, Ezra and Nechemiah	184
Abraham and Esther - Parallel Points of Origin	186

END OF NIGHT

The Final Dawn	191
The Last Hope	193
Glossary, Biographical Notes and Historical Chart	195

Dayan Ch. Ehrentreu
Av Beth Din Europe

בס"ד

חנוך הכהן עהרנטרייא
אב בית דין אירופה ומלפנים בלונדון

55 SHIREHALL PARK
LONDON NW4 2QN
TEL: +44 (0) 20 8202 2364
FAX: +44 (0) 20 8203 8942
Email: dayan@ehrentreu.com

ששת הימים 41
רמת אשכול
ירושלים
טל: +972 (0)2 532 8551
פקס: +972 (0) 2 532 8552

ט"ו בשבט תשע"ח לפ"ק
31. 1. 2018

I deem it a privilege and a pleasure to write a הסכמה to the latest book of Rabbi Akiva Tatz שליט"א entitled " As Dawn Ends The Night " . Rabbi Tatz is a תלמיד מובהק of the late Rabbi Moshe Shapiro זצ"ל and a lot of the material in this book he has culled from his שיעורים . The material refers to the changes that have occurred in many spheres of life since the אנשי כנסת הגדולה.

Rabbi Tatz is a prolific, eloquent writer, and has had a tremendous influence on people all over the world both young and old, whose lives have vastly changed and now look at life from a תורה perspective.

May Rabbi Tatz be blessed with good health to ensure that he continues to disseminate תורה values for many years to come.

Ehrentreu

Dayan Ch. Ehrentreu

Acknowledgments

This book was written in the shadow of the passing of Rabbi Moshe Shapira, our generation's teacher. Almost everything presented here derives from his teaching. Now that we have lost him, the gifts he left us are assuming proportions larger than life. Among the most valuable of those gifts is the clear light he taught us to focus on principles: in every area he showed how to identify the key issue or the core idea, the underlying fundamental, the root.

As he demonstrated in so many ways, the details are not nearly as important as the rule, the *reason* that generates those details. Wisdom lies not in knowing the details but in understanding why they *must* be the way they are. Real wisdom requires driving down to the deepest layer of cause; fathoming the single underlying principle that explains all.

One of the principles that he illuminated is the subject of this book. It is a key principle in Jewish history that unlocks many mysteries; time and again he would use it to explain perplexing areas of Torah, masterfully wielding it over the years to tease out and clarify thread after golden thread in the tapestry of Torah and Jewish history as a unified conceptual framework took shape before our eyes. When seeking his approval while preparing the material for the book I ventured to comment that I had chosen this theme because of its explanatory power: he had shown us how many areas of Torah make sense only in its light. When I said that there must be twenty subjects like that, he responded: "Twenty? Two hundred!" and that was the end of the conversation. I was clearly on the right track.

I have presented the central thesis in a relatively stark way for the sake of clarity, but as the book progresses a more complex and nuanced picture will emerge.

I am indebted to a number of people for invaluable help. Rabbi Jeremy Kagan, a student of Rabbi Shapira's inspired by the potency of the theme developed here, set down its essential features in his books *The Jewish Self* and *The Choice to Be*. I have benefited from those works and from his comments on this one.

Rabbi Marcel Bordon has been a pivotal guide, constantly opening doors in my learning in general and facilitating access to Rabbi Shapira's Torah in many ways. His contribution to this book has vastly improved it.

Rabbi Gavriel Tatz produced the detailed historical chart. I hope readers will find it useful beyond its function as an adjunct to this book.

I have gained from the teaching of Rabbi Dovid Gottlieb and Rabbi Abraham Hassan over the years and over the course of this book's evolution. For important help I would like to thank R. Yehuda Dombey of Targum Press, my sister Mrs Anna-Louise Shapiro, Tamar Tatz and Zelig Kirzner.

Working with Rabbi Danny Kirsch, Rabbi Benjy Morgan and the staff of the Jewish Learning Exchange, London's branch of the Ohr Somayach family of institutions, continues to be a privilege. They have provided the forum for learning and teaching within which the book developed.

Jonathon Triest and his family have made this book's publication possible; their refinement and generosity are admired and appreciated.

My wife Suzanne is the real reason that this book has seen the light of day. She could very well be described as the dawn that ends the night.

A.T.
Shevat, 5778
February, 2018

Preface

Connection to a higher world seems almost hopeless to us; we do not even know what a real connection might look like. It is not that we have lost it; we feel as if we never had it to lose. We long for a point of connection; if only we could witness a miracle, or perhaps hear a prophet speak... but those things are no more than distant memories. We feel the space of centuries setting us apart from their reality.

As we try to warm ourselves by that distant fire, we wonder - why is the world this way? Why is a vibrant spirituality that was once clearly central to human experience now only a story?

And is there any way to bring that ancient story to life?

I:
The Fading of History

Chapter 1

Light to Darkness

When a famous astronomer was asked why he was an atheist, he answered: "Because I see God everywhere in the Bible and nowhere in the Universe."

This is a serious challenge; it requires analysis and deserves a response. Torah reflects the world; or more accurately, the world reflects Torah - since Torah is the "genetic program" underlying all of reality, the world *must* reflect Torah. Every word in Torah codes for an aspect of the world. In fact, the Hebrew word for "word," *davar,* is the same as the word for "thing" or "object" because every thing in the world is a projection of the Divine word that brings it into being. Whatever is in Torah must be in the world; whatever is in the world must be in Torah.[1] *"Istakel ba b'Oraisa u'bara alma* - God looked into the Torah and created the world" (Zohar 2, 161a); the world is a copy of the Torah. If God is seen everywhere in Torah, He should be seen everywhere in the world; things could not

---

[1] If one knows Torah, one knows the world, and vice versa: Abraham observed all the Commandments although he lived before the Torah was given - he deconstructed the world to discover its underlying source in Torah down to the finest details. King Solomon, who lived after the giving of the Torah, looked into Torah to plumb the depths of the world: the Midrash (Tanchuma, Kedoshim 10) states that he grew crops in Jerusalem that do not ordinarily grow there - he delved into Torah to discover the lines of energy that run from Jerusalem to every part of the world, and on the lines that run to distant lands he planted the crops that grow in those lands, and they grew in Jerusalem. Torah can be deduced from the world; the world can be revealed through Torah.

possibly be otherwise if Torah is true. This is the basis for our astronomer's assertion – if Judaism claims that whatever is manifest in Torah must be manifest in the world, we have a serious inconsistency: Torah is full of God – He appears to His prophets and speaks to them openly, and those conversations are the fabric of Torah. In addition to prophecy, He reveals Himself in miracles throughout Torah (in fact these phenomena go together: a miracle occurs only in the presence of a prophet - see page 88).

So wherever you look in Torah you see God, but no matter where you look in the world, you do not see Him. It would seem that one of these - Torah or the world - must be deceiving. Our astronomer explores the world and finds it devoid of God's manifest presence, so he concludes that it is the Torah that is mistaken. That is the logical process that forms his atheism. To him, God is a claim that is not supported by the evidence.

Why does Torah describe a world that appears utterly unlike its description? The answer to this question will not demonstrate God in the world; indeed He is not visible here. But it will show why the Torah and the world do not appear to match; why God is manifest in Torah but hides in the world - *despite the Torah's claim that it parallels the world exactly.* Understanding the solution to this problem is a key to understanding all of Torah and all of history.[2]

First, the principle of the solution in broad outline:

History comprises two phases – the phase of the revealed *(gilui panim)*, followed by the phase of the hidden *(hester panim)*. From the Creation until approximately two thousand three hundred years ago, God appeared

---

[2] The Torah does not mention the Resurrection of the Dead or the World to Come. The Oral Law derives their existence from textual clues, but the Torah never mentions them explicitly. There are many reasons for this (see Kli Yakar, Devarim 26:12 for seven classic explanations; there are more) but one suggested by Rabbi Aharon Kotler illustrates our point precisely. Rabbi Kotler pointed out that since a basic axiom in Torah is that the world parallels the Torah exactly, whatever is hidden in Torah must be hidden in the world, and whatever is revealed in Torah must be revealed in the world. If the existence of the World to Come were revealed in Torah, *it would be revealed in the world.* If the world is to hide its final destination (so that it remains *another* world and not simply a part of this), that transcendent dimension must be hidden in Torah. Things could not be otherwise.

openly in the world. Then, during a period that centers on the era of the Great Assembly, He receded into hiding and a second phase of history began, the phase of concealment. Torah was written during the first phase; Torah is in fact a contemporaneous documentation of that revelation, capturing in its text the progression of that phase as it occurred. And when that phase of history ended *Torah fell silent.*

The Written Torah runs parallel to the world it describes; it shows God everywhere because He was visible everywhere. As God spoke to prophets and revealed the miraculous, Torah describes those phenomena; Torah is precisely their record. When the phase of the revealed ended, written Torah ended. When God retreated behind the mask of nature, a veil was drawn over Torah. The Torah that continued in the subsequent darkness, veiled and opaque, is the Oral Law.

"God is everywhere in the Bible and nowhere in the Universe." Exactly. The Bible is precisely the written record of God's appearance in history. When that appearance ceases, Bible ceases. *The Torah and the world match exactly* – when the world reveals, Torah reveals. When the world hides, Torah moves into the mode of the Oral Law, a mode of derived wisdom, a wisdom that no longer shines visibly but speaks from behind a mask. When the spiritual is visible, Torah captures that revelation. When the spiritual is hidden from view it must be heard by a sensitive ear inclined in the darkness. The Written Law is the Torah of a prophetic and miraculous world; the Oral Law is the Torah of a purely natural world, a world in which the spiritual is far from obvious.[3] *"Achen ata El mistater....* You are a God Who hides" (Isaiah 45:15).

("You are a God Who hides" - this is true throughout history. Isaiah is stating that even in his prophetic era there were times of revelation and times of relative obscurity. Even in the prophetic era God was not openly visible to everyone at all times and places; He manifested from time to

---

[3] The Written Torah *does* in fact contain all of history, including post-Biblical history and all of the Oral Law; but it does so in coded form ("[All] that a veteran Sage will later expound... was already given to Moses at Sinai;" Yerushalmi Peah 2:4; and see Vilna Gaon on Avot 1:1 for further sources). Torah encompasses everything, it is the genetic material of all that exists in space and time; nothing could exist in the world if it were not in Torah. The entire span of history *must* be there. And indeed it is; but the first phase of history is explicit in Torah, while the second is coded in textual clues that require deciphering.

time in miracles. The point, however, is that the *mode* of those centuries was revelation: constant prophecy and intermittent miracles made the world luminous in a way that is incomprehensible now.)

Over a period of some thousand years, more than a million prophets arose among the Jewish people.[4] Prophecy was openly available and prophets were easily accessible - the natural response to misplacing a possession was to ask a prophet where it could be found (Samuel I; 9:6-19). God Himself was available in that phase of history, He was the natural address for any need: the natural response to illness was to consult a prophet to learn the spiritual root of the illness or to turn to God directly - King Asa was punished because he consulted physicians instead (Chronicles II, 16:12).[5]

We can no longer relate to that degree of revelation as real. (Indeed, in some ways we are prohibited from doing so: it would not be genuine for us - see below, page 142). A world in which no effort was needed to discover the Divine has become a world in which great effort is needed to find conclusive evidence. A world once glowing with spirituality has become opaque.

Our astronomer knows the Bible. If it is written by the hand of God, surely it must be a description of the sum total of all reality. Surely this Book must be complete in every way; a master plan and open description of all history. What could be more obvious? But that is not correct; the Bible extends from Genesis until a particular period in history, the period of the last prophets. And then it is silent; when there are no longer prophets to receive Divine dictation and write it down, there is no more dictation. A new phase begins, a post-Biblical era in which the mode of Divine communication is utterly different. The Written Law ceases; the Oral Law takes over. Our astronomer is unaware of that; and unless he engages the Oral Law and immerses himself in its rigorous training of perception, he will never know.

---

[4] The *gemara* (Megilla 14a) mentions 48 prophets and 7 prophetesses. It then proves that there must have been more and asks why only these are counted? The *gemara* answers: "There were more, as it is taught: 'Many prophets arose among the Jewish people, twice as many as the number [of Jews] who left Egypt (600,000), but only prophecy that was required for future generations was written down; prophecy that was not required [for the future] was not written.' "

[5] See p142 for more on this.

The Men of the Great Assembly presided over that historic transition. More than that: to a large degree, they engineered it. This book traces that change, their role in crafting it, and some of its broader consequences.[6]

The Modern Mind

The change could hardly have been more sweeping. Nothing escapes the effect of that event; it sets the nature of our consciousness and colors our perception of the entire modern world. It sets the stage for all of modern life; the very structure of the mind and all that is possible - and impossible - in modern thought are its results.[7]

The modern intellectual worldview is the product of the transition from an essentially religious vision of the world to a secular one. That was the central change, and we cannot escape its effects. Our modern minds are formed in a materialist mold and we cannot think ourselves out of it because the tools of our thought are secular. We see the world in a particular way: modern scientific reductionism frames the only view we have. We are no longer able to relate to the spiritual as real.

We cannot relate to prophecy; it is out of our range. We do not see it as real because it is out of our experience. Our minds have shrunk, our cultural view is the result of a smaller consciousness. The vision has changed because the one seeing has changed. We are locked into this; there is no way out of it for us because the tool that might liberate us is part of the prison. We cannot think our way out of our intellectual and cultural world while the tool of our thought itself is part of that world.

In fact, the choice to see the world in materialist terms is itself a statement of faith; there is no objective reason for it but it is accepted because the spirit of the age obliges it.

---

[6] The pre- and post-Great Assembly periods are also denoted as First Temple and Second Temple eras. After the destruction of the First Temple, prophecy continued for a while: living prophets remained, but no new prophets arose. By the time of the Second Temple, prophecy was over.

[7] See J. Kagan, The Jewish Self (Feldheim 1998) and The Choice to Be (Feldheim 2012) for extended discussion of this theme.

Honest materialists concede that their commitment to materialism is not based on evidence but is a profession of faith. Here is a frank statement by a leading evolutionist:

> "Our willingness to accept scientific claims that are against common sense is the key to an understanding of the real struggle between science and the supernatural. We take the side of science... because we have a prior commitment, a commitment to materialism. It is not that the methods and institutions of science somehow compel us to accept a material explanation of the phenomenal world, but, on the contrary, that we are forced by our *a priori* adherence to material causes to create an apparatus of investigation and a set of concepts that produce material explanations, no matter how counter-intuitive, no matter how mystifying to the uninitiated. Moreover, that materialism is absolute, *for we cannot allow a Divine Foot in the door*" [italics added]. (Richard C. Lewontin; The New York Review 1997)

Materialism dominates totally; nothing could be more reasonable to the modern mind. Things *must* be this way after the change - *daat* or inner wisdom is not seen as real; any construct that is not based exclusively in materialist philosophy or validated in a laboratory is not taken seriously. Knowledge or experience arising from the spiritual dimension is regarded as irrelevant or even delusional; at best a mere epiphenomenon.

Modern materialist science operates within a paradigm created in the void that remained when the spiritual faded from view. In the modern world, science is the only arbiter of what is true.

All this is a result of the change that the Men of the Great Assembly presided over. Prior to that era, things of the spirit were real. Inner knowledge was real knowledge; the world glowed with prophetic clarity and the world of empirical science merely provided practical tools. Reality was defined by the deepest wisdom; science was a servant. But after that era, it has become a master. Science presumes to define reality, and in a world without prophecy it has no real competition.

The ending of prophecy marks the transition from the period of revelation to the period of hiddenness (from *gilui panim* to *hester panim*). In order to understand this transition, its importance and its far-reaching consequences, some background is necessary.

Chapter 2

Decline of the Generations

The ending of prophecy was a watershed event in history. It was not simply one phenomenon among others, merely a detail; rather, it marks *the major transition* in Jewish and world history. The ending of prophecy represents a juncture in history that is not just a further step in the decline of the generations, but a singular, categorical change. *Yeridat hadorot* (the Decline of the Generations) is a phenomenon permeating history; each set of generations is lower than the previous in spiritual potential and greatness. However, this particular descent was greater not only in degree but in kind. If the other steps represent a dimming of the light from one era to the next, this step represents the transition from light to darkness. Previously the changes were measured in varying shades of light, now they can be measured only in degrees of groping in darkness. At that point in Jewish history the lights went out...

As we move away from Sinai through history, the intensity of spiritual experience drops. The blazing clarity of the Sinai revelation fades with each step of transmission.[8]

---

[8] The revelation of kabbalistic wisdom *increases* over history - more is revealed as time goes by. See Leshem Sh'vo v'Achlama (Klallim, *klal* 2, *anaf* 3:9). For the descent over history and the hidden *tikkun* (correction) effected thereby, see Shaarei Leshem 271-277.

"If the earlier [generations] were angels, we are men, and if the earlier [generations] were men, we are like donkeys... and not even like the donkey of Rabbi Chanina ben Dosa or Rabbi Pinchas ben Yair [whose donkeys behaved in extraordinary ways] but like ordinary donkeys..." (Shabbos 112b).

"As gold compares to dust, so our father's generation compares to us..." (Yerushalmi Gittin 6:7).

"The hearts of the early Sages were like the doorway to the Entrance Hall [of the Temple, which was twenty by forty cubits], and the hearts of the later Sages were like the doorway to the Sanctuary [which was ten by twenty cubits]. And we [our hearts] are like the eye of a fine needle" (Eruvin 53a).

"The fingernail of the earlier [generations] was better than the belly of the later" (Yoma 9b).

"With the next generation the heart became diminished and things that had been simple to the earlier [Sages] and which had been clear to their students... became subject to doubt..." (Rav Sherira Gaon, Iggeret).

"[Regarding] the diminution of prophecy and wisdom generation after generation... the prophets and sages in sequence are like a chain of causes and effects, which as they become distant from the first cause diminish in degree..." (Rabbenu Nissim, Derashot).

"The [earlier] generations were better and more righteous than the later... it is impossible for the later to be like the earlier" (Rashi; Rosh Hashana 25b).

This diminution proceeds in stepwise fashion - a long plateau lasting some centuries is followed by a steep drop, another plateau is established, and another drop follows. We are now in the set of generations known as the Acharonim - the latter or "last" set. This age has endured from the 16th century to the present; prior to this, broadly speaking, from the 11th to the 15th centuries, was the age of the Rishonim, or "first" (relatively) set. Prior to that were the Gaonim (9th - 10th centuries) and prior to that the Amoraim (authors of the Talmud; 3rd to 5th centuries), and prior to them the Tannaim, or Mishnaic authorities. Before the period of the Mishna, prophecy was manifest - and ended around two thousand three hundred years ago.

The general process is a devolution from head to feet; the earliest generations were the "head" of Jewish history, the last ones, the feet. In fact, our set of generations is referred to as *ikveta d'meshicha,* or the heels of the Messianic form.[9]

The decline over history is not simply a matter of shrinking of the intellect; it affects the entire human form - the decline is not in what people *know* but in what people *are*. The descent over Jewish history is only part of a supernally greater process - the journey of mankind as a whole that began at a level close to the Divine. Adam was cosmically great; he spanned the Universe (M. Rabba 8:1). He inhabited the entire Universe, he was immortal, and the angels were unable to discern him from the Divine (M. Rabba 8:10; *"Vatachserehu me'at me'Elokim* - You made him only slightly less than God" - Psalms 8:6). The light that shone from his lifeless heels *after* his fall and death was greater than the sun (B. Batra 58a). But he was drastically shrunk ("God put His hand upon him and shrank him..." - Sanhedrin 38b). Even then, his dimensions were gigantic, and he lived for almost a thousand years. The generations that followed were far greater than the present scale; Leshem calls them the *"arich anpin"* (kabbalistic reference to transcendent root level) of the human state; people of those eras lived for centuries and were of a stature far above our ability to grasp. After the Flood there was a major downward shift; the post-Flood human stature was immeasurably lower than before. Lifespans fell drastically, to the *"ze'er anpin"* (reference to a far lower spiritual level) of history. After the Dispersion (during the generation of the Tower of Babel) in Abraham's day, the world fell again, to the proportions that begin to resemble those that are familiar to us.

---

[9] At the present stage of history we are as devoid of sensitivity as the thick dead skin of the heels. (And like the heels are dead to pain but sensitive to tickling, we are insensitive to the worst immorality and brutality but available for superficial stimulation that produces empty laughter - Rabbi Moshe Shapira.)

The Vilna Gaon writes that when Isaiah (52:2) calls to the lifeless final pre-Messianic generation of Jews to "Shake yourself off and arise from the dust" he does not mean from the dust where you are, but from the dust *that* you are (Likutei HaGra 136-137).

Thus there were three tiers in the hierarchy of generations: from Adam to Noah, from Noah to Abraham, and from Abraham onwards. According to the esoteric tradition there are three spiritual parts to the human form, both at the individual and the cosmic levels: *neshama, ruach* and *nefesh*. *Neshama* is essentially transcendent, in and above the head, and links the human to the spiritual worlds; *ruach* is the center of human experience, located in the heart, and *nefesh,* represented by the lower body and the legs, is the link to the body, the animal and the material world. The ten generations from Adam to Noah corresponded to *neshama,* the ten from Noah to Abraham to *ruach,* and from Abraham onwards, to *nefesh.*[10]

That is the story of the devolution of man from Adam to the present day - a spiralling down from a being who held the Universe in his God-like consciousness to a creature who sees himself as the utterly meaningless result of an accidental biological process, literally an animal.

Life's Two Phases
In general, life experience comprises two phases: the first is inspired and perfect, but temporary. The second is much lower, but real and lasting.[11] The purpose of the first phase is inspiration, "charging up" as it were; the second is the phase of challenge in which the work is done, drawing on the stored charge of the first. In the second, what would be impossible without the inspiration and the momentum of the first can be done. The first phase sets the goal; the second phase is the journey to reach that goal. No meaningful journey can be undertaken unless the destination is first specified, and yet of course merely specifying a destination achieves nothing. Both are necessary: clear definition of destination and then the unrelenting work of the journey that must be taken to translate that vision into a destination that is real.

---

[10] Rabbi Shapira. That is why Torah was given to the later generations: the purpose of Torah is primarily to elevate and sanctify the *lower* aspects of the human - mitzvot are physical actions perfomed in the material world for that purpose.

[11] Living Inspired (A. Tatz, Targum Press, 1993) describes the phenomenon of first and second phases as a general principle. This book examines the particular historical change from revelation to hiddenness to show that all our current experience is a function of our position deep in the second phase of history.

These two stages correspond to the spiritual qualities of *chessed* and *din*. *Chessed* is the root of going toward, connection, relationship; *din* is the root of withdrawal, disconnection, separation. It is essential to understand that in the mode of *din*, with all its difficulty and sense of detachment, there is a great benefit: independence is born here. Cutting renders asunder, severs, casts the receiver away from the giver. But for the price of that pain of separation, the receiver acquires himself. Precisely when the child is weaned, he gains independence. The comfortable closeness is lost, that is the price; but the gain is freedom and the maturity of independence. This is the greatness of the kind of charity that gives the receiver the dignity of independence rather than the shame of continued dependence. The verb used for giving kindness is *"gomel"* - as in *"gomel chessed."* But the literal meaning of *gomel* is to wean, which is a withdrawal and a withholding, the opposite of giving. This seems totally inappropriate; but the meaning of this phrasing is clear: in the act of weaning a deeper kindness is manifest than in the act of feeding.

This paradox is sharply expressed in the second blessing of the *amidah* (prayer service): the blessing relates to the quality of *din*, severance, detachment or withholding. This quality is usually associated with death, the severance from life; it is Esau's quality - and Esau lives by his sword. Yet the subject of this blessing is life: the blessing ends with the words "Who revives the dead." Again, this appears entirely inappropriate. But the meaning here is that precisely when the receiver is cut off from the giver, the receiver achieves life - an independent life of his own. Revival of the dead, the ultimate form of life that is not subject to death, is generated precisely by the quality of *din*.

The second phase of history, the phase of darkness in which revelation and transcendence are out of sight, makes our own creative work possible. The price we pay is our distance, our detachment from God. The benefit we gain is our independent ability to create; at this distance from the Source, we have room to move. Of course this is dangerous; amplified human free will is dangerous in the extreme. But more free will means more potential for assertion of our own originality.

Male and Female Create Together
The first phase is male; the second female. The male contributes the spark of conception, the female brings it into reality and gives it independent

life. He is all potential,[12] she converts potential to actual. He is all unbounded energy, she sets bounds;[13] he generates all that might be, she converts that unlimited potential into the finite reality that a finite world can hold. The world of possibilities is endless, anything *could* be; but the world of reality is always limited - the final crystallization into hard fact requires the sacrifice of fluid potential for just this particular reality to manifest.

In an ideal world the female expresses all the male's potential. All that is conceived is born; all that *could be* conceived is born. In the real world that is not the case. Originally sun and moon were equal: the moon reflected all the sun's light. The verse (Genesis 1:16) states: "The two great luminaries..." - they were equally great, no hint of difference is indicated. Later however, the verse states: "The great luminary to rule by day, and the small luminary by night..." A drastic change had taken place. Originally, states the *gemara* (Chullin 60b), when sun and moon were equal, the moon objected: "How can two rule with one crown?" God responded by instructing the moon to diminish herself. In the world that resulted, the reflection is always incomplete, often only the pale shadow of a brilliant source. The world did not begin that way: the original state was ideal - the world reflected its Source perfectly; later the world fell.

The meaning of this sequence is that perfection is the original state; things begin that way because that is true and right, the ideal is set up first as it must be - that is origin and it must be destination. Then, secondarily, a fall takes place; things break down. That fall is where the receiver gains the potential - the power and the privilege - to strive for growth to perfection. That is where the receiver gains independence; that is where free will is generated. And that is where real danger lurks, disaster

---

[12] The Hebrew word for "male" is *zachar;* cognate with *zecher,* memory. In *gematria* the word *zikaron,* a memory, is equal to *zera,* a seed - precisely the male role in conception: a seed is no more than the compressed memory of previous generations given by the male for the female to express in the world.

[13] The Hebrew word for "female" is *nekeva;* the literal meaning of this term is to make specific, as in the verse that states *"asher nikvu b'shemot* - who were specified by name." Or as in *"nakva alai s'charcha v'etena* - Fix your wages and I will pay you;" that is, give me a specific number so that I can pay you. A payment cannot be made until a sum is specified. Infinite potential must be converted to the limited actual before a thing can exist in the world.

becomes possible - that is the price. But that is where the prize becomes real too - a reconstructed world built by the genuine independent effort of vulnerable creations. The moon has shrunk, but it will be great again.

Male potential and female actualisation are required for creation. "All things in the world are [composed of] male and female" (Zohar 3, 290b). The father begins; the mother completes. That is the sequence of creation.

That is the basic pattern of all reality. All of history is a repeating cycle of these two phases, spiralling down over time.[14] Just as male and female together create a new reality, these two phases of history create the living being that is Torah. Each first phase inspires its second; each first phase provides the conception that the second develops. But at the largest scale there are only two: the first set of centuries of revealed light, and the second set of darkness. First, the phase of Divine revelation, prophecy and its crystallisation in the Written Law. Then the second, the phase of translating that inspiration into a new form; a darkness in which the challenge is to re-ignite from within the world a clarity that was once given from Above. The effect of the two phases is to build the ultimate partnership: the Divine beginning with Creation and reaching a climax with the giving of the Torah, carried to its completion by the human integration of that lost light in the Oral Law. Understanding these two phases of history gives a deep insight into the nature of the Oral Law and its remarkable meshing of Divine and human wisdom.

Written and Oral Laws Both Rooted in the Written

Ultimately all of reality is located in the Written Law; it is the source, it must contain all of Torah, and therefore the roots of the Oral Law are found there too. All that will come to be expressed in the Oral Law, including every opinion of every Sage who will live later, has a source in

---

[14] There were two sets of Tablets - the first were Divine, entirely miraculous; the second had to be carved by human hand.

There were two Temples - the first manifested revelation, clarity and *Shechina* (the Divine Presence); the second Temple lacked those. The second Temple was an empty shell compared with the first - those who had seen the first wept when they saw the second (Ezra 3:12 and Rashi there).

The third Temple will be a return to perfection - the end goal is always a return to original perfection, via the effort that is necessary to build it.

the Written Law (Yerushalmi Peah 2:4). Within the Written are the latent elements of the Oral, waiting to be brought to light and developed by human genius over the centuries. The transition from Written Law to Oral Law is presaged in a number of ways within the Written:

The first four books of Torah comprise direct dictation from God to Moses; the Giver speaks and the receiver hears and records. The fifth book, Devarim, however, begins with the receiver - Moses utters his own words, and God ratifies them as Torah.[15] Here, man speaks and God agrees - exactly the style that the Oral Law will later establish.[16]

At another level of refraction of this pattern, the last eight verses of Devarim are of a different kind than the preceding text from Genesis until that point - the *gemara* states that these last eight verses include a contribution from Joshua. Here is clearly a transition from one level to another, from master to disciple. These verses are authored jointly by teacher and student; again, precisely the mode that will define the Oral Law.[17] Indeed, the entire Book of Joshua and the entry into the Land of

---

[15] See Zohar 3, 261b; Ohr HaChaim beginning of Devarim; Malbim explains that God commanded Moses to write as the book of Devarim what Moses had said earlier of his own accord. (Cf. Ramban Devarim 5:12; Ohel Yaakov quoting Vilna Gaon; R. Y. I. Chaver, Ohr Torah on the nature of the Book of Devarim.)

[16] See page 56: *"Lo bashamayim hi* - It is not in Heaven."

[17] The last eight verses of Torah describe Moses' death. Obviously, Moses could not truthfully have written "And Moses died..." In resolving this problem the *gemara* (B. Batra 14a-15b) presents two opinions: Moses wrote those verses *"b'dema"* - usually translated as "in tears," or alternatively, Joshua wrote them. The Vilna Gaon (Kol Eliyahu, V'zot HaBracha 133) asks: how does writing "in tears" justify the falsehood? And to suggest that Joshua wrote verses in Torah is highly problematic - the whole Torah is the "Torah of Moses." The Gaon's answer is that both opinions are true - together. *"B'dema"* can mean "mixed," or unseparated (just as tears blur the distinct clarity of vision): Moses wrote those verses in a continuous string of letters not separated into individual words (as in the primordial Torah written, according to kabbalistic tradition, before Creation). After Moses' death, Joshua separated the letters to reveal the words describing his master's death. So both are true: Moses wrote those verses *"b'dema,"* and Joshua had a hand in them too. The point that relates to our issue is that these verses are transitional: written by both master and disciple.

These eight verses also hint to a later addition: the eight days of Chanukah (see below page 163 and page 169).

Israel that it documents is given as another source for the Oral Law within the Written (R. Zadok HaKohen, Likutei Ma'amarim 1).

A later version of this pattern as it develops through Torah: Mishle, the Book of Proverbs, presages the second phase of Torah. Mishle means "metaphor;" here King Solomon gives metaphors in place of the real, analogies in place of the actual. The value of a *mashal* (analogy) is that it explains the real where the real is too distant. The price is that one is no longer in contact with the real; the benefit is that one comes to understand it. King Solomon is translating the original into a tool in the hand of the user: "He tied rope to rope and thread to thread, drew up the deep waters and drank, and [made it possible for] everyone to draw and drink..." (Shir HaShirim Rabba 1:8; see there for further *mashalim* for King Solomon's writings). Torah is too deep to grasp in this world; Mishle brings it closer to hand, like the rope that brings water up from a deep well. Again, this is precisely the mode of the Oral Law that brings Torah within reach and translates it into practical application.

Mishle is written in the prophetic era; indeed, it is part of Scripture, but it is essentially the wisdom of Solomon.[18] In giving metaphor to reality, Mishle represents a transition from Divine prophecy to inspired human wisdom.

There are other points of origin of the Oral Law within the Written:[19] the second Tablets were crafted by Moses - God wrote upon them but Moses had to prepare them; a human hand was required. All that would later become the Oral Law was *written* on the first Tablets (Bet Halevi Part 2, *drush* 18) - all was written and clear, all of Torah could be simply read.

---

[18] King Solomon is himself "transitional" - he comes after the seven personalities who define the span of Torah (Abraham, Isaac, Jacob, Moses, Aaron, Joseph and David). David is the last; his son Solomon is the first of a new order. Solomon lives within the prophetic era but he lays down the root of the second phase by "connecting rope to rope and thread to thread" to arrive at the distant truth, just as the Oral Law makes the connections needed to arrive at the meaning of Torah. King Solomon's Song of Songs is also an extended metaphor (a metaphor that transitions across extremes - expressing the highest of spiritual connections in the earthiest of terms). His Eshet Chayil (Woman of Valor) too, is a metaphor on many levels. (The letters of "Shlomo" also spell *"hamashal"* - the metaphor.)

[19] R. Zadok HaKohen, Pri Zadik 5, 21 and Resisei Layla 128 on Devarim as source; see Likutei Ma'amarim 1 for the book of Joshua as source.

No effort of interpretation was necessary. But those were broken; what survived for future generations was the Torah of the second Tablets. In effect, the process of intense effort required to master the Oral Law is the work of reconstructing those broken Tablets.

When Moses struck the rock to extract its waters instead of speaking to it he generated a world in which Torah can be extracted only by blows (Tikkunei Zohar 44b). Had he spoken, the world would have revealed Torah in response to every request; now Torah reveals its meaning only through great exertion. Torah was originally open in the world, its deepest messages available for the asking. Now its understanding requires blows; many layers of resistance in the human heart and mind must be beaten into submission before Torah can be heard. That is the work of engaging the Oral Law, a process that is all extreme effort.

Origin and destination, potential and actual. All of Torah manifests this pattern: heaven and earth in the first verse; the first four books and the last; all of Torah and then the last eight verses; Torah and Mishle; first and second Tablets - there are endless expressions of the pattern. And in the broad sweep of history, the first phase reveals in prophecy and miracle, the second hides in nature.

The step-wise decline of the generations is a general principle, it pervades Judaism. Some stages of decline were minor, others major. The step down from the prophetic to the post-prophetic era presided over by the Men of the Great Assembly was probably the most precipitous step in history.

Chapter 3

Knesset HaGedolah - The Great Assembly

Who were the Sages of the Great Assembly?

The Great Assembly (Knesset HaGedolah) was a convocation of Sages and Prophets from the last years of the Biblical to the early Greek period around two thousand two hundred years ago.[20] It included the prophets Chaggai, Zechariah, Malachi (Ezra), Nechemia and Daniel. Chananya, Mishael, Azarya,[21] Mordechai and Zerubavel were also members. The Great Assembly, sometimes designated as "Ezra and his Bet Din (Court of Law)," spanned the era that saw the end of prophecy - Chaggai, Zechariah and Malachi were the last prophets. Shimon HaTzaddik,[22] who

---

[20] "Ezra's court is called the Men of the Great Assembly; they were Chaggai, Zechariah and Malachi, Daniel, Chananya, Mishael and Azarya, Nechemiah ben Chachaliah, Mordechai, Zerubavel; other Sages were with them, numbering altogether one hundred and twenty. The last of them was Shimon HaTzaddik who was included among the one hundred and twenty and who received the Oral Law from all of them; he was High Priest after Ezra." (Rambam, Introduction to Mishneh Torah).

[21] Chananya, Mishael and Azarya - see page 182.

[22] Shimon HaTzaddik: in his days the daily miracle of the Menorah occurred sporadically (Yoma 39b); the phase of miracles was drawing to a close.

saw those prophets, was one of its "remnants." Shimon HaTzaddik confronted Alexander (Yoma 69a); the end of the Great Assembly era was the beginning of the Greek.

Maharal (Pirkei Avot 1:1) notes that after the Great Assembly, Torah was contained and transmitted first by individuals, then by pairs *(zugot)*, then again by many. The Knesset HaGedolah was *knesset* in essence - a unified gathering.[23] They established that mode, the perfect totality of a composite Torah, and they passed that Torah to one individual (Shimon HaTzaddik). He too passed that on, but the ongoing decline then reached a level at which no single individual could contain all of Torah. The *zugot* took over, each member of a pair holding one half of the body of Torah,[24] until finally no pair was great enough to contain it, and Torah split into a multiplicity of open possibilities and debated positions from which a reconstructed truth must emerge - the version of the Oral Law that we have today.

The first Mishna in Pirkei Avot (Ethics of the Fathers) states:

> "Moses received the Torah from Sinai and transmitted it to Joshua; and Joshua to the Elders, and the Elders to the Prophets, and the Prophets transmitted it to the Men of the Great Assembly. They [the Men of the Great Assembly] said three things: 'Be deliberate in judgment, raise many disciples, and make a fence for the Torah.' "

Maharal asks many questions about the precise wording of this Mishna. Among his questions are these:

1. Why does the Mishna begin its detailing of the process of Torah transmission with the term "received," and then switch to the term "transmitted"? And further, why does the Mishna continue its use of the

---

[23] An "Assembly" - it comprised numerous individuals, but it was united; it was the beginning of a transmission that depends on a multiplicity. It is precisely the unity and harmony of that multiplicity that sets the tone of the Oral Law; the Oral Law is a unification of parts that combine to construct the truth. At the level of the Great Assembly the unity was complete; argument crept in later.

[24] One member of each pair representing the right side *(chessed)*, and one the left *(din)*: Nasi and Av Bet Din respectively, together encompassing the whole (Maharal).

term "transmitted" until the Great Assembly, and then (in Mishna 3) resume use of the term "received" ("Antigonos of Socho received from Shimon HaTzaddik...;") and so on, using that term exclusively to document the transmission of Torah through the successive generations?

2. Why does the Mishna introduce the term "transmitted" a second time in describing the handing of the Torah from the Prophets to the Great Assembly ("the Prophets *transmitted* it to the Men of the Great Assembly"), but finds it unnecessary to specify "transmission" in describing the previous two stages (from Joshua to Elders and from Elders to Prophets)?

3. Why do we find no teachings (*mussar,* moral teachings) from the Prophets or from the Elders, while we do find such teachings from the Great Assembly ("They said three things: Be deliberate in judgment, raise many disciples, and make a fence for the Torah")?

The answer to the first question, says Maharal, is that "receiving" and "transmitting" are terms that relate to the receiver and the transmitter in terms of their respective powers: when a body of wisdom is transmitted, it is these powers that will determine the completeness of the process. "Transmitting" is the appropriate term to use when the transmitter gives over *all* the contents of his message, and that can happen only when the receiver is able to receive all; but when the receiver is deficient relative to the transmitter, then the term "receiving" must be used because the amount transmitted will depend solely on the receiver's (limited) capacity. Therefore the Mishna begins with "Moses received the Torah" because no human being could possibly receive the whole Torah (an expression of the infinite); Moses received what a human could receive and no more. The limiting factor here is entirely on the part of the receiver; it is the receiver's capacity that determines how much will be transferred, and therefore the term "received" must be used.

However, when Moses transmits the Torah to Joshua, he is able to transmit all that he has and Joshua is able to receive it all. There is no deficiency on the part of the transmitter or the receiver; therefore all the wisdom of the transmitter can be transmitted, and the term "transmitted" is appropriate. The same applies to the next stages of transmission: from Joshua to the Elders, from the Elders to the Prophets and from the Prophets to the Great Assembly. All these stages of transmission were complete: all that the transmitter had to give was received by the receiver.

The Torah was handed down fully and accurately in the chain stretching from Moses to the Great Assembly.

But from the time of the Great Assembly, things changed. Says Maharal: "From the Men of the Great Assembly, the generations began to decline and shrink." Therefore when the Mishna continues describing the chain of transmission beyond the Great Assembly (in Mishna 3) it states: "Antigonos of Socho received from Shimon HaTzaddik..." Here the term "received" is re-introduced because the transmission is again limited by the capacity of a (deficient) receiver. And that term is used for all the successive stages of transmission described by the Mishna, each stage's passing on of Torah defined not by the giver whose power is unlimited in giving but by the receiver whose limited capacity defines the efficiency of the process. The decline of the generations takes on major significance after the era of the Great Assembly; from that point on Torah cannot be transmitted whole. Each successive generation, smaller in spiritual capacity than the previous, can receive only what its limited vessels can hold.

After the Great Assembly the generations' power to receive diminished precipitously. As Maharal quotes: "Rabbi Eliezer the Great said: 'I learned much from my teachers, and yet all I took from them [in proportion to their wisdom] was as much as a dog licks from the sea...'" Until the Great Assembly, giver and receiver were matched. All that Moses had to give was received by Joshua; he in turn passed on all that he received to the Elders. Through the Prophets that transmission continued with no attenuation. The Great Assembly received it all. And then the decline began: each generation receiving from the previous only a small fraction of the wisdom of its teachers.

The answer to the second question (why the term "transmitted" is mentioned again explicitly in the step from Prophets to the Great Assembly) states Maharal, is to emphasize that this is where that chain of perfect transmission ended. That sequence began with "transmitted" and it ends with "transmitted;" from here on, the passage of Torah from teacher to student through the generations will be subject to the declining potency of history.[25]

---

[25] Maharal shows why the transmission from Moses to the Great Assembly required each of those five particular steps and why those stages were not subject to diminution (see Maharal, Derech Chaim, Machon Yerushalayim 5767 with notes by Y. Hartman).

In response to the third question (why the Great Assembly found it necessary to teach three *mussar* principles while the previous generations of Elders and Prophets had simply transmitted Torah with no added teachings or advice of their own), Maharal says this: the Men of the Great Assembly saw that wisdom was waning. Although in their generation Torah was still intact, they saw that such clarity could not last. In fact, three generations after the Great Assembly (Shimon HaTzaddik received from the Great Assembly, Antigonos received from him, and Yosef ben Yoezer and Yosef ben Yochanan, the first of the *zugot* or pairs, received from Antigonos) the first unresolved argument crept into the process of transmission (see pages 69-72) and from that time on the greatness of individual Torah authorities diminished palpably. The *gemara* (Temura 15b; see Rashi there) puts it thus:

> With the death of Yosef ben Yoezer... and Yosef ben Yochanan... the *eshkolot* (individuals who encompassed the entire Torah) disappeared. All [those individuals] among the Jewish people from the days of Moses until the death of Yosef ben Yoezer learned Torah like Moses our teacher. From then on, they were not able to learn Torah like Moses our teacher... All [the great individuals of those eras] who arose among the Jewish people from Moses until the death of Yosef ben Yoezer contained no imperfection. From [Yosef ben Yoezer and Yosef ben Yochanan] on, they contained imperfection.

When the Great Assembly "saw that the intellect was progressively weakening," states Maharal, and that the generation "no longer had a firm grasp on wisdom," they acted to prevent damage in the same way that a doctor prescribes appropriate measures to compensate for a physical weakness or malady. Maharal goes on to explain in detail why in such circumstances there are three areas of weakness in particular that require such measures and how each of the teachings of the Great Assembly was designed to address one of them. In various ways, as Maharal shows, *mussar* teachings that are intended to support Torah and Jewish life had become necessary; until then there were no vulnerabilities that needed attention and therefore there were no "therapeutic" measures taught by the Elders or the Prophets. The Great Assembly instituted protective and defensive teachings for the first time because they had become necessary.[26]

---

[26] See page 54 for another fundamental insight into "They said three things..."

The Men of the Great Assembly were uniquely placed and uniquely qualified to take those steps. Maharal explains that they shared characteristics of both the prior and the subsequent stages: although in their time the light had not yet dimmed - Torah was still being transmitted intact - they were no longer transcendent in the way that Prophets (and of course the Elders) were. Prophets exist on a different plane; in a sense they are superhuman. A prophet's consciousness is not of this world, he lives in a higher dimension. The members of the Great Assembly, however, were "merely" human; indescribably great to be sure, able to relate to prophets and receive Torah with no deficiency, yet they were no longer personally living in the rarefied atmosphere of the supernatural.

Maharal is demonstrating how the Mishna delineates in the clearest terms the categorical change that began with the Great Assembly. The Men of the Assembly saw what was coming. They stood at the brink of a plunge into the gathering darkness; and while they yet lived in daylight, they perceived its approach and prepared the Jewish people to enter it.

The Great Assembly was in essence transitional, Prophets and Sages together ("a hundred and twenty Sages and among them a number of Prophets"), and its task was managing transition. Reaching back to the Written Law for seeds of conception and reaching forward to give birth to the Oral Law, the Sages of the Great Assembly were its midwives.

Understanding this transition is the key to understanding its consequences. Many themes in Torah and events in history make sense only in its light. Some of those are:

Historical Transitions and their Consequences
- Spiritual worldview replaced by materialist worldview
- Prophecy ends, Scripture sealed
- Atheism replaces idolatry

The Oral Law and the Power of the Sages
- The Oral Law
- The Sage is greater than the Prophet - *Chacham adif mi'navi*
- The creative power of the Sages
- "They said three things..."
- "The world stands on three things..."
- Argument and dissension in the Oral Law

- Mutually exclusive Torah statements are both true - *Elu v'elu*
- The sealing of the Talmud
- The Sages and scientific error

New Modes of Being
- Breakaways and reforms
- Miracles cease
- Blessings formally composed
- Prayer: formal liturgy composed
- Language: Hebrew no longer the Jewish vernacular
- Seeing and hearing
- Beauty: the vessel of virtue becomes a tool of temptation

New Festivals, New Torah
- Purim
- Certainty becomes doubt
- The new work of faith
- From rebuke to flattery
- Greece: the new nemesis
- Science and miracles
- Chanuka: the festival of the Oral Law
- Prophets may not add to Torah
- Tisha B'Av - why the mourning lessens

Personalities of Transition
- Chananya, Mishael and Azarya parallel Abraham, Isaac and Jacob
- Daniel, Ezra and Nechemiah

This is the map for the chapters that follow. The Men of the Great Assembly stood at the fulcrum of history; these are the things that they instituted, directly or indirectly, and that shape our experience in the modern world.

II:
Historical Transitions

Chapter 4

The Closing of Prophecy
- from Idolatry to Atheism

The drive to worship idols was once almost irresistible. That is no longer the case; nowadays we do not crave idolatrous worship. What caused this fundamental change in the structure of the human spirit?

The *gemara* (Yoma 69b; Sanhedrin 64a) states:

> And they [the men of the Great Assembly] cried out in a great voice to God. What did they say? Rav, or according to others Rabbi Yochanan, said: "Woe, woe! It is this [the Evil Inclination for idolatry] that has destroyed the Temple and burned the Sanctuary and killed all the righteous ones and exiled Israel from their land, and still it dances among us. Did You give it to us for any reason other than to receive reward [in overcoming it]? We do not want it and we do not want its reward!"
>
> A note fell to them from Heaven, on which was written "True." (Rav Chanina said "This implies that the seal of the Holy One, Blessed is He, is 'Truth.' ") They fasted for three days and three nights, and it [the Inclination for idolatry] was delivered to them.

> It emerged like a fiery lion from the Holy of Holies. The prophet [Zechariah; a member of the Great Assembly] said to Israel: "This is the Inclination for idolatry," as it is said: "This is the Evil One" (Zechariah 5:8). As they seized it, a hair fell from its mane, and it raised its voice in a roar that went out over [an area of] four hundred *parsaos*. They said: "What shall we do?"... The prophet replied: "Cast it into a leaden cauldron and cover its opening with lead."

Thus the Great Assembly exorcised the drive for idolatry from the human psyche. Idolatrous practices that survive today are merely superstitious remnants, customs performed to honor ancient traditions (*"Minhag avoteihem beyadeihem* - Continuing their forefathers' customs" - Chullin 13b). Today there is no natural innate craving for that worship, and it is impossible for us to understand the drive to worship idols.[28]

From our position in history, locked into a psyche formed in the image of materialism, we cannot relate to prophecy or the craving for idolatry in any real way. For us, these are purely theoretical. The concept of a human driven almost uncontrollably by an urge to subjugate the self to something that appears to us a mere fetish or lifeless totem appears unintelligible. Since that drive was removed from the world, we cannot relate to it as real.

The *gemara* (Sanhedrin 102b) puts it thus:

> Rav Ashi said to his students: "Tomorrow we will begin the lecture about our colleagues [the sinful kings, including Menashe; referring to Menashe and his idolatrous contemporaries as "our colleagues" was a pointedly disparaging reference]." Menashe appeared to him in a dream and asked [indignantly]: "You call us your colleagues and your father's colleagues?" [Menashe proceeded to ask Rav Ashi a halachic question.] Rav Ashi replied: "I do not know [the answer]." Menashe retorted: "You do not know the answer [to this question] and yet you call us your colleagues?" Rav Ashi said: "Teach it to me and tomorrow I will cite it in your name during the lecture." [Menashe then taught Rav Ashi the law].

---

[28] See J. Kagan, The Jewish Self (Feldheim 1998) and The Choice to Be (Feldheim 2012).

Rav Ashi [humbled by Menashe's superior knowledge] asked: "If you were so wise, why did you worship idols?" Menashe answered: "Had you been there you would have gathered up the hem of your cloak and run after me [to idolatry]." The next day, Rav Ashi said to the students: "Let us begin with our teachers..."

Menashe's generation was far superior to Rav Ashi's. Menashe lived in the era of prophecy; his generation's vision and depth of Torah knowledge surpassed Rav Ashi's beyond measure. *And its temptations were commensurate:* the greater the power of good, the greater the power of evil - energy available for good will drive with equal force and produce equivalent damage when diverted to evil. When great spiritual wisdom is attainable the world must contain a counterbalancing force: human free will must always be poised at the balance point of real freedom.[29] When genuine worship is passionately craved the passion for idolatry will be almost irresistible. Menashe taught Rav Ashi that his generation had worshipped idols because their temptation was greater than many could resist; Rav Ashi, had he lived then, would have gathered up his cloak in the most undignified way to run after idolatry with total abandon. He would have been no match for the temptation. The greatness of Menashe's generation had not protected it from idolatry - on the contrary, *that greatness was the reason* for its temptation.

Rav Ashi had been oblivious to the power of that ordeal. He lived at a time when nothing could have seemed simpler than resisting the foolishness of idolatry. But he was living after that passion had been surgically excised from the human heart; Rav Ashi and his contemporaries no longer possessed that faculty. The Great Assembly had excised it precisely because it had become almost irresistible. "Did You give it to us for any reason other than to receive reward [in overcoming it]?" At a time when humans could vanquish it, overcoming its temptation was a rich opportunity for reward. But now that it conquers us more than we conquer it "We do not want it and we do not want its reward."

Rav Ashi realised that vastly greater personalities had been subject to vastly greater ordeals. Where he had spoken disparagingly of Menashe

---

[29] See A. Tatz, Will, Freedom and Destiny - Free Will in Judaism (Targum Press, 2014) for a full discussion of the point of balance of free will and its shift over history.

before, he was now forced to acknowledge his superiority ("Let us begin with our teachers...").

The temptation for idolatry had been central in human consciousness; it lived at the very heart of human motivation. When the Great Assembly called it up "It emerged like a fiery lion from the Holy of Holies" - that is where it dwelt; at the deepest and holiest level of the human mind and soul, where the flames of the deepest motivations burn.

By Rav Ashi's time, the temptation of that area had become trivial. What was once an almost irresistible passion seems a mere caricature to us now.

Idolatry
To understand this phenomenon further it is necessary to understand the nature of idolatry itself.

The common conception of idolatrous gods is that they are no more than figments of fertile imaginations. But the Torah relates to them as if they are real - many verses refer to gods other than God as if they are very real indeed: "Who is like You among the *gods,* Hashem (the Name)?" "For all the *gods* of the nations are small gods;" "For Hashem is a great God and a great king over all *gods."* Who are these "other gods"? If they are mere fetishes, surely the appropriate injunction should be: "Do not get involved in falsehood; do not attribute reality where there is none."

Moreover, the Torah uses names for these "other gods" that are names of God. *"Elohim acheirim"* (other gods); *"eilim"* – these names are profane versions of authentic Divine names. Names are of essence in Torah; why are false gods referred to by the same names as God Himself? One would expect the Torah to use names for idolatry that convey the idea of empty illusion.

Further, the Torah's greatest prohibition is idolatry; this is the first of all the negative commandments ("You shall have no other gods before Me..."). If idolatry were no more than foolishness it would be enough to say: "Do not be gullible." The root prohibition of the Torah must surely be posed against something real.

What is the meaning of bowing in worship to a physical object? Who would carve a statue and then bow down to the work of his own hands asserting that it has a power beyond his own - why would sane people do such things? What was so desperately sinister about idolatry and why was the drive for it so powerful that it had to be eradicated from the world before it wrought irreparable damage?

Idolatry must be taken more seriously than simply dismissing it as primitive nonsense. In the sources of idolatry lurks something very real. In essence, the idea of idolatry is relating not to the supernal Source of all existence *but to the channels that bring down from that Source* into the world. An idolater focuses on the zodiac (the "worship of stars and zodiac" is the common Torah terminology for idolatry) or on the forces of nature: sun, moon, stars, wind, rain. His graven images are tangible representations of these (ancient idolaters did not regard their physical idol as an absolute source of reality but as a focus in the world of some higher power, imbued with its own magical energy derived from that power).

Maimonides (Laws of Idolatry 1:1) states that originally, close to the beginning of history, people acknowledged God alone. Then came a stage when they reasoned that since He uses agencies such as sun and moon to operate in the world, it must be fitting to give honor to these as His emissaries. They began to accord honor to the intermediaries as well as to God, and eventually they remained focused on the channels only:

> In the days of Enosh people made a great error. The advice of the wise of that generation was annulled and Enosh himself was among those who erred. This was their error: they said "Since God has created the stars and zodiac to conduct the world, and He has placed them in the firmament and given them honor, and they are agents that serve Him, it is appropriate to praise and glorify them and give them honor. This is God's will - to honor and give greatness to those that He has honored and given greatness just as it is a king's wish that those who serve him are honored. Since this was their concept, they began building temples to the stars and to offer sacrifices to them and to praise and extol them and to bow to them in order to reach God's will, following their mistaken opinion. This, in essence, was idolatry. They did not claim that there was no God other than [their particular] star... Everyone knows that You alone are God; their mistake and their foolishness was that they imagined that this was Your will.

Rambam goes on to describe how, with the passage of time, God was omitted from the picture and eventually forgotten by all but a handful of individuals.

It is clear that idols are interposed between humans and God as intermediaries (or their symbolic representatives). In Guide for the Perplexed (1:36) Rambam states:

> Those who worship idolatry do not worship it thinking that there is no God other than it; none of them ever imagined that a form made of metal or stone or wood created heaven and earth and controls them. However they worship an idol as a representative of the [agent or power that they see as] intermediary; it [the agent or power that the idol represents] is intermediate between them and God... and no observer of Torah can argue with this.

Looking to those intermediaries is indeed looking in the direction from which all higher energy comes into the world. But looking *no further* than them is idolatrous – a correct perception looks beyond them to their Source, realizing that they are mere agents. The foolishness and emptiness in idolatry is the belief that the intermediaries have any *independent* power.

The "other powers" of idolatry are not imaginary; those forces of nature are the transmitters of Divine energy into the world. Their names are derived from His because they are indeed the channels that emanate His manifestation into the world. What is false about them is the notion *that they are sources in their own right*.

The drive to idolatry was the extreme longing to transcend the self in connecting to a greater reality. The faculty that lies at the root of human consciousness that strives to transcend, to draw the human upwards into an expanded version of the self is the faculty that craves idolatry. It craves the experience of worship because worship correctly understood is a striving to connect to a higher reality. Worship is not only a prostration that demonstrates lowliness. It is the forging of a bond between the receiver and the Giver. That is in essence exactly the worship of God. The error in idolatry is not in the concept of worship but in the failure to transcend to the Source; idolatry reaches beyond the self *but it does not go far enough*.

The idol worshipper reaches out to the proximate sources, the channels that bring down what he wants and needs in the world; he is not focused on the ultimate Source because at heart he is interested in his own needs. Who supplies those needs is irrelevant to him. The root of his fault lies in the ego and self interest; the idolater is prepared to subjugate himself and pay the price that idolatry requires - to serve his own interests. At the deepest level, idolatry is worship of the self. It is a craving to transcend, but at root it is unable to detach from the ego.

End of Idolatry, End of Prophecy
Prophecy and idolatry are fundamentally linked. It is no accident that when idolatry was banished from the human psyche the ability to experience prophecy died simultaneously. The part of the mind that craves idolatry (its root and interface with transcendence) is the same part that receives prophecy. This faculty "transmits" and "receives" - in terms of "transmission" it longs to move beyond itself and project the self outwards and upwards, high into that rarefied zone in which it can make contact with a higher reality. In terms of "receiving" it is the faculty that is sensitive to the voice of prophecy; it is the very same part of the mind that can hear the voice of the Absolute.

This is the faculty of communication with the higher world. The correct application of that drive is Divine service, its incorrect form is idolatry; they are the correct and incorrect uses of the mode of projection. This faculty can experience the ecstasy of prophecy, but it is open to seduction by the lure of idolatry.

This is the reason that the *yetzer* or drive for idolatry came flaming from the Holy of Holies. It lives at the root of the mind, at the center of the psyche, its point of attachment to a higher world.

When two aspects of the mind share a common origin they stand or fall together. The price of removing one must be loss of the other. This is illustrated by considering the next step taken by the Great Assembly after they eliminated the drive for idolatry: the *gemara* goes on to say that, seeing that their efforts were successful, the Great Assembly proceeded to weaken the drive for male-female intimacy in an attempt to end illicit relationships. It soon became apparent, however, that the price would be unacceptable: for days no fresh eggs could be found. (Without the natural drive in this area, chickens had stopped producing eggs - Rashi observes that even eggs *already within the bodies* of chickens were not laid: the world had so cooled that even eggs already formed ceased their incubation.) That signified risking the end of humanity - eliminating the male-female desire from the world would indeed end illicit relationships, but it would also end all procreation. The Great Assembly were obliged to reinstate that essential drive, but they tried to do so in a controlled fashion: they requested that from then on, a man should crave a relationship with his wife, but with no other woman. Their effort was met with a message from Above that "halves are not possible" here: that drive either exists or it does not. This is not a craving that can be modified to discern appropriately.[30]

When an organ is removed from the body, *all* its functions are lost; when a faculty is removed from the psyche, all its functions must be lost too. Idolatry and prophecy are functions of the same central faculty, and when one goes the other must go too.

A Darker World
The loss of prophecy leaves mankind disconnected. The existence of prophecy in the world does not mean only that individual prophets could be found; when prophecy existed *the entire world* lived on a higher plane. In the age of prophecy, beyond the individuals who had attained that state *the world at large was more illuminated*. Individual prophets could attain their level only because they represented the pinnacle of a corporate body, the Jewish people, that was high enough. The heads of the people are always organically connected to the body, the people. As the body moves up, the head moves up; when the body moves high enough those gifted and developed individuals are lifted into the realm of prophecy. When the body falls the head falls too; if the body falls far enough even the greatest will fall below that defining line and no-one will experience prophecy.[31]

---

[30] The Great Assembly did, however, achieve partial success: they were able to "blind" the male-female drive in such a way that a man should not crave an intimate relationship with his close relatives - it is now not natural for a man to feel an intimate attraction to his mother or sister.

[31] When the Jewish people sinned, God said to Moses: *"Lech red ki shichet amcha* - Go down for your people have sinned." When the people descend, Moses must descend even though he had no part in their sin. In similar vein, a Heavenly voice announced that Hillel the Elder (and later, Shmuel HaKatan) was "fit for the Divine Presence to rest on him" - but that his generation was not worthy (Sanhedrin 11a). When a generation falls short even its greatest individuals are bound by its limits.

When prophecy disappeared, the entire world darkened. Now no-one can see what was visible before. When prophets lost their prophecy, ordinary people lost spiritual insight. The world has become darker for all. The central problem of our era is spiritual deficiency. What was obvious before has become the problem of faith.

Atheism Replaces Idolatry
When prophecy and the drive to idolatry ended, an emptiness remained. Idolatry has been replaced by atheism. Idolatry is too much spiritual awareness (misguided in the extreme, but driven by an intense craving); atheism, too little.

After the connection to Source is severed, the craving to transcend remains focused on the highest it can – and that highest is now within the self; since transcendence is no longer possible, the desire must be for self. In the first phase ego is expressed in idolatry, in the second as the fixation on self that atheism may cultivate. When prophecy and idolatry go, an empty space remains that can be occupied only by ego. In the phase of atheism, the only choice that remains is between the existential vacuum of total nihilism or the sense of self as total.

***Tikkun* of the Power of Idolatry**
Man's detachment from the Source of prophecy is disastrous; he moves into a void in which he can hear only his own voice. Yet that disaster makes possible its own solution: the Oral Law becomes possible. In the phase of the Written Law the work is to hear God's voice; in the phase of the Oral Law our work becomes to discover our own. The detachment that manifests as atheism in which man is the only measure of what is real also makes possible the process of deciding independently in Torah. Independence works both ways: it means a lonely detachment with no direct connection to Source, and yet that very detachment allows the independence of creative thought that is at the heart of the Oral Law. Detachment from a life source risks death, but it is a necessary step to create independent life. While the seed is attached to the tree it is alive with the tree's life; it is no more than a part of the tree. When it falls to earth it loses its life connection and in fact begins to decay. But in that process of decay the miracle of independent life sparks, and if the delicate new shoot survives it too will become a tree, able to propagate further life as an independent part of an endless process.

The desperately wrong response to discovering independence from God is to assert that independence as the atheistic ego that assumes mastery of its own reality. The correct response is to use that very independence to create a Torah that is new and yet totally loyal to the original. The essence of the Oral Law is its independence, its freedom to assert its own opinions - *"Lo ba'shamayim hi...* It is not in Heaven."[32] Its goal is to create Torah through the independent genius of its exponents to reach an entirely new creation, and yet to reveal in that new creation nothing that is not derived from the original that has gone into hiding.

The brazenness of idolatry that sets up an alternate reality can equally well be asserted as the aggressive independence of mind that characterises the Oral Law.

Only in this phase of detachment far out of range of the last echoes of prophecy could the independent reality of an Oral Law be created. The very detachment that invites the egotistical assertion of atheism makes possible the sublimation of that independence into building the magnificent structure of a Torah that expresses the sharp originality of its masters. In that world distant from Divine clarity a Torah comes into being whose exponents create it with a deftness and certainty of touch that allows them to outvote God Himself (and paradoxically evoke His approval)[33] - the astonishing channelling of a potentially atheistic *chutzpa* into a sacred Torah of human fashioning that will eventually reach history's final destination.

---

[32] See below page 56.

[33] See below pages 56-57.

III:
The Oral Law and the Power of the Sages

Chapter 5

The Oral Law

The second phase of history gives us the opportunity to become creators. That expansion of free will can be used wrongly to take the world further from its Source, or used correctly to begin the process of its return. Atheistic ego detached from all Godliness, or development of an Oral Law using that same independence of mind to reveal Godliness in the world. Argument and dissension that break down Jewish unity, or the "argument for the sake of Heaven" characteristic of the Oral Law that paradoxically builds unity.

Torah takes two forms: the Written Law which was given during the era of prophecy and the Oral Law which is developed by man in the post-prophetic phase.[34]

The Oral Law becomes possible precisely because of the independence of the second phase of history from its Biblical origins. This is the change from *navi* to *chacham* - from Prophet to Sage; and it is the reason that the Sage has an aspect of superiority over the prophet *(chacham adif mi'navi)*.[35]

---

[34] The Mishna, the definitive repository of the Oral Law, was also given at Sinai. It was passed down orally in parallel with the Written Torah. But when prophecy ended, the creative human component within the Oral Law began. That began what is properly called the phase of the Oral Law (see below).

[35] See below page 61.

Prophecy is a voice from another world speaking with an intensity beyond our imagination; an intensity so great that it leaves our voice all but inaudible. When prophecy withdraws, a spiritual silence descends upon the world, a night in which our voices carry far. During the phase of the Written Law, which is co-extensive with prophecy, man receives with clarity, there is no place for his own creativity in the sense of creating Torah; that would be absurd.[36] You cannot see more clearly than when God shows you.

The Written Law leaves no room for independent human expression within Torah. We have no record of any original statement made by any prophet in the chain of Torah transmission during the years of prophecy. The reason is not that they were not creative enough but that their Torah was given clearly; their work was not to create Torah but to receive it and transmit it. When a prophet speaks he speaks God's words – *"ko amar Hashem... thus says God."*[37]

They Said Three Things
When the Men of the Great Assembly inaugurated the phase of the Oral Law, the Mishna which records that inauguration begins: *"Hem amru shlosha devarim –* They said three things..." (Avot 1). This may appear to be nothing more than an introduction to the words of these Sages, merely a reference. In fact it is a momentous declaration: in this simple statement the secret of the Oral Law is being announced. *"They* said three things..." – the import of this statement is that until now no-one said anything, that is, no-one said anything *of himself,* no-one within the Torah tradition created Torah of his own; to the extent that he was identified with the transmission of Torah the Prophet transmitted God's Torah purely and clearly, but now that God is no longer speaking openly the realm of independent human expression in Torah begins. *"Hem amru shlosha devarim..."* for the first time in history transmitters of Torah spoke Torah

---

[36] Moses could not relate to Rabbi Akiva's Torah (Menachot 29b). There is no place for the creative work of resolving doubts when all is clear.

[37] It is true that each prophet speaks *in his own style;* the individual personality of the prophet refracts his message uniquely (only Moses adds no style of his own - his perception is through an absolutely "clear lens" - Yevamot 49b). Indeed it is a principle of prophecy that no two prophets speak identically (Sanhedrin 89a). Despite that, however, the prophet speaks God's words. That is not the case when the Sages speak - see below.

of their own; these statements are *theirs*, no longer solely the direct transmission of a Divine dictation. From now, the transmitted wisdom of Torah that the Mishna contains will be what the Sages say. All that had been said in Torah to that point was a transmission of what had been received; from here it includes an element of original creation.

From that time on all Torah is recorded in the name of the Sage who says it, not merely for the politeness of attribution but because *he is an intrinsic part of what he teaches*.[38] Torah is now part of the heart and mind of the Sage who utters it.[39] From now the sayer is part of what is said. When codifying what constitutes heresy against the Oral Law, Rambam (H. Teshuva, 3:8) conflates denial of its statements with denial of the status of its personalities: *"V'hamak'chish magiddeha* - And one who impugns [the Oral Law's] Sages:"

> There are three [categories of those] who deny the Torah: one who says that the Torah is not Divine, even one verse or even one word... And similarly one who denies its explanation, which is the Oral Law, or one who impugns its transmitters [the Sages]...

One who attacks the person of a Sage of the Talmud attacks the Talmud. The Sage and what he expresses are *both* essential components of the Oral Law; they cannot be separated. The statements of the Oral Law do not stand outside of their authors; the two are meshed in the deepest way.

Previously, Torah was God speaking; the Prophet listened.[40] Now the Sage speaks his own mind, and that mind is Torah. This is the radical

---

[38] From now, the transmitter is an integral part of the transmission - the Talmud not only gives the name of the relevant Sage for any particular teaching ("Said Rabbi Akiva..."), it gives a string of attribution ("Said Rabbi Yehuda in the name of Rav..."), and sometimes a lengthy string - three or four authorities in sequence, each citing the sources before him.

[39] A common expression in Talmud when introducing the opinion of a Sage is: *"aliba d'...;"* for example *"aliba d'Rabbi Akiva..."* The meaning here is "according to the opinion of...," but the literal meaning is "according to *the heart of...*" that Sage. The central locus of his Torah is not his mind or his thought but his *heart;* the Sage's opinion is of his essence, he and his Torah are inseparable in principle.

[40] Now, amazingly, God may do the listening: "God fulfils the decrees of the righteous" (Tanchuma Vayera 19; also Moed Katan 16b; Zohar Genesis 45).

shift of the latter phase of history. Mishna and *gemara* are a record of *the statements of particular human beings* no longer transmitting Torah as a frictionless conduit for its pure content. They are now originating that content themselves with all the labor and creativity that effort demands. God's Torah has become man's. Of course it is created only upon the base of the Torah which is transmitted, without that it would not be authentic; so that there is now a seemingly impossible combination of Divine transmission developed with total dedication to that transmission, a body of human creation that expresses the Divine.

The Oral Law is the shimmering creation of human intellect and opinion that no longer has access to explicit Divine revelation, yet acting in complete consonance with Divine opinion.

This is exactly the operation of the Oral Law. Torah is now what the Sages say it is.[41] [42]

Lo Ba'Shamayim Hi - It is Not in Heaven

There is a further step in this paradoxical relationship: from now on, even if there were a revelation of Divine opinion *it would be overruled by human opinion*. This is the principle of *"Lo ba'shamayim hi* – It (the Torah) is not in Heaven." The classic discussion of this principle is the *gemara* (Baba Metzia 59b) that documents a particular *halachic* debate among the Sages:

The majority, led by Rabbi Yehoshua, held one view; Rabbi Eliezer held another. Rabbi Eliezer attempted to convince the majority that he was correct, but was unable to do so. He proceeded to prove his point thus:

> "If the law accords with me, let the carob tree prove it." A carob tree uprooted itself and moved. The Rabbis responded: "We do not bring proofs from carob trees." Rabbi Eliezer said: "If the law

---

[41] Maharal on Avot 1:1 (p111 in Y. Hartman annotated edition).

[42] The Oral Law exists only while in flux - while an aspect of Torah is under discussion and the debate is in process, the Torah is an "Oral Torah;" once the discussion crystallises into a *halachic* conclusion, that piece of Torah takes on an aspect of the Written Torah. Oral Torah is oral; it lives only in the creative dynamic of its development (Rabbi Moshe Shapira).

accords with me, let the stream of water prove it." A stream of water reversed its direction and began to flow uphill. The Rabbis said: "We do not bring proofs from streams of water." Rabbi Eliezer continued: "If the law accords with me, let the walls of the study hall prove it." The walls began leaning. Rabbi Yehoshua admonished the walls: "If the Rabbis are arguing halachic matters, what does that have to do with you?" The walls ceased falling in deference to Rabbi Yehoshua, and remained suspended in deference to Rabbi Eliezer (and they are still leaning). Rabbi Eliezer said: "If the law accords with me, let me be vindicated from Heaven." A Heavenly voice announced: "Why do you dispute Rabbi Eliezer? The law accords with him in every case." Rabbi Yehoshua rose to his feet and said: *"Lo bashamayim hi...* It is not in Heaven" (quoting Devarim 30:12). What is the meaning of "It is not in Heaven..."? Rabbi Yirmiya said: Since the Torah has already been given at Sinai we are no longer obliged by Heavenly voices because You wrote in the Torah at Sinai (Shemot 23:2): "Follow the majority opinion..." Rabbi Nathan subsequently encountered Elijah the Prophet and asked him: "What was God doing at that time (when the Heavenly voice was outvoted)?" Elijah answered: "He was smiling and saying: 'My children have defeated Me, My children have defeated Me.' "

Rabbi Eliezer proved his case with miracles and a Heavenly voice. Those are tools of the prophetic trade. They may be appropriate for a Torah that is "in Heaven," but they are ruled out of order in the world of the Oral Law; in that world *"Lo bashamayim hi* - It is not in Heaven." At an absolute level, there is no doubt that Rabbi Eliezer was correct. But that is not the reality of the Oral Law; at the level of the Oral Law, Torah is in our hands and its rulings are decided by us.[43] Such an approach would have been unthinkable during the era of prophecy: in that era we were in contact with the Absolute and nothing less was meaningful. Now that we have no connection with an absolute truth we must construct it ourselves.

---

[43] To be sure, we create and decide in Torah only according to its principles: Rabbi Yehoshua and his majority outvoted the Heavenly voice only in obedience to the Torah principle of "Follow the majority opinion." When the principles themselves are subject to human manipulation, that is neither Written nor Oral Torah but illegitimate distortion.

In his commentary to the Talmud, Arizal asks a strange question here. Of all the things he could have probed in this remarkable discussion, he asks this: Why does the *gemara* say of Rabbi Yehoshua that "he rose to his feet"? What does that add to the meaning of his statement that the Torah is not in Heaven? Had he remained seated would his words have been any less significant? Why is this apparently trivial detail mentioned?

Before giving Arizal's answer, some background is necessary. The first phase of history corresponds to a supernal "body;" the second to "legs." All structures in the world have a human form; both space and time follow that pattern. The human body ends where the legs begin - the legs are referred to as *"l'bar mi'gufei,"* external to the body. The function of legs is to carry the body from one place to another; they are not part of the body proper, only its vehicle. The organs of reproduction end the body; where the parent ends, the child begins. In fact, in Torah a child is designated as a "foot" of the parent: *"bra kara d'avuha"* ("the son is the foot of his father") - meaning that the father "walks" into the future in his child; the child takes the father from the present into the future just as the legs carry the body to a new place. In the internal system, the ability to reproduce is known as the spiritual qualities of *netzach* and *hod;* these are the right and left aspects of the origin of the process of reproduction. In the external system, *netzach* and *hod* are the right and left legs, respectively (Patach Eliyahu).

Netzach means "eternity;" this is the quality that generates eternity - children continue the lives of their parents, and since the children themselves will produce further children, the process is potentially eternal.

In the span of history, the post-Biblical festivals of Purim and Chanukah are designated *netzach* ("eternity") and *hod* ("glory"). They come after the body of Torah ends; they are added on, external to the main body of Torah history. Purim and Chanukah are of Rabbinic origin; they are essentially festivals of the Oral Law. They extend Torah when its open revelation ceases; they give it historical eternity. Purim and Chanuka are the "legs" of history.[44]

---

[44] Shaar HaKavanot, Shaar Rosh Chodesh. See below page 165.

This apparently insignificant line in the *gemara*, says Arizal, is the key to the entire discussion. Rabbi Yehoshua rose to his feet to state that the Torah is not in Heaven because this is precisely the point in Torah history where we take over; from here on, the enterprise of Torah becomes ours. From here, *we stand on our own feet*. Torah has moved beyond the body to the zone of the legs. Parent gives way to child here; the process of eternity is asserted. That is also the deeper meaning of the *gemara's* statement *"nitzchuni banai,"* usually translated as "My children have defeated me...;" but an equally accurate translation is "My children have given me *netzach,* eternity..." From here I walk on them, so to speak; My Torah is now the ongoing creation of the Jewish people as they move through history. My children are my vehicle, they carry me in the world; they are my chariot.

Later Generations do not Argue with Earlier Ones
One of the features of the decline of the generations is that later authorities do not argue with earlier ones in Torah learning and ruling (in general). When the *gemara* (B. Batra 170b) records Rav (an Amora) overruling a Mishnaic source, Rashbam comments: "Rav is a Tanna and therefore he can argue." Rashbam clearly understood that an Amora cannot argue with the Mishna; this *gemara* therefore requires explanation - how could Rav dismiss the opinion of Tannaim? Rashbam's answer is that Rav's status is transitional between Tannaim and Amoraim (Rav was one of the very earliest Amoraim) and that gives him sufficient Tannaic status to disagree with a Tanna. From this discussion it is apparent that Amoraim do not argue with Tannaim. Later generations do not argue with earlier ones. There is a learned discussion about the precise limits of this convention,[45] but the general principle applies - as the generations descend, later authorities yield to earlier ones.[46]

Rabbi Elchanan Wasserman (Kovetz Shiurim 633) demonstrates that there are in fact cases of Amoraim arguing with Tannaim. He records that

---

[45] See Rosh (Piskei HaRosh Sanhedrin 4:6) who shows that later authorities can in fact disagree with earlier ones *within the same set of generations,* among other conditions that govern the general principle.

[46] Rabbi Y. Kamenetsky (Emet L'Yaakov, Beha'alotecha) shows that the pattern of strict deference shown by each generation to the previous is not merely of conceptual value: it is fundamental in the process of halachic ruling in practice.

he asked Rabbi Chaim of Brisk how this could be, and that Rabbi Chaim answered that Amoraim could indeed argue with Tannaim, *but they chose not to*.[47]

(Rabbi Simcha Wasserman pointed out that Amoraim very seldom made original *drashot* - halachic derivations - on verses in the Torah, thus tacitly demonstrating the superior level of the Tannaim who routinely derived laws in that way.)

This principle of yielding authority to earlier generations takes on special significance with the sealing of the Talmud. There is a categorical difference between the authority of the Talmud and all subsequent opinion. On the statement of the Rama (Choshen Mishpat 25) that a judge may rule against an earlier decision in a matter that is *not* in the *gemara*, the Vilna Gaon comments that rulings of the *gemara* cannot be overruled, as the *gemara* itself states (Baba Metzia 86a): "*Rav Ashi v'Ravina sof hora'a* - Rav Ashi and Ravina (final editors of the Babylonian Talmud) are the final authorities."[48]

Can a Later Authority Answer the Question of an Earlier One?

On occasion, we find a later authority answering a question left unanswered by an earlier one. This seems problematic: if the earlier generations were greater, how could a later (and lesser) authority solve a

---

[47] Rambam (Hilchot Mamrim 2:1) states that a later Bet Din can argue with an earlier one because we are obliged "to follow the Bet Din of your generation." On this the Kesef Mishna asks: So why do Amoraim in fact not argue with Tannaim - according to this Rambam they have authority to do so? Kesef Mishna answers that "From the day of sealing of the Mishna they accepted upon themselves that later generations would not argue with earlier ones. And from the time of sealing of the Talmud no-one may argue with it."

There is a difference of opinion about the exact meaning of this Kesef Mishna. Rabbi Chaim Brisker (see above) understands that Amoraim *chose not* to differ with Tannaim out of respect for their senior status. Chazon Ish (Likkutim Hilchot Mamrim) understands that they did not argue because *they knew they were incompetent* to do so. Either way, there is a clear break in levels of authority from one stage to the next.

[48] See page 75 for a discussion of the critical change that occurred with the sealing of the Talmud and its consequences.

problem that defeated an earlier one? This issue is raised, for example, when an Acharon answers a question that a Rishon leaves open. It is axiomatic that a Rishon would have known any answer that could be suggested by an Acharon, and therefore if he did not offer it himself, it must be deficient. What is the correct understanding of these cases?

The general approach is this: the answer given later is indeed deficient, and that is precisely why it was not suggested by the Rishon. But at the level of the Acharon, its deficiency is no longer clear. He gives an answer where none was forthcoming before *because of his limitation.* An analogy may help:[49] Two men are trapped in a locked room; one has vision, one is blind. The sighted man sits passively making no attempt to escape. The blind man begins carefully feeling the walls until eventually he finds a narrow opening which he manages to squeeze through and escapes. Now we may ask: how is it that the one with limited abilities escaped while the one with more did not? The answer may be this: the blind man escapes because all he can do is feel the crack in the wall, so he takes his opportunity and leaves; but the sighted man remains *because he sees through the crack and sees that the situation outside is worse than inside.* It could be that when an earlier authority chooses to ignore a tempting solution to his question, he does so because his superior vision detects that the solution raises more difficulties than it solves. The lesser authority cannot see that; he sees the immediate solution and he offers it. Of course he does so with all humility - very often when an Acharon proposes a solution to the problem of a Rishon he begins with the humble admission: "If not for the fact that this answer was not suggested by [the relevant Rishon], I would have proposed..." and then goes on to give it. There are exceptions; we do find Acharonim arguing with Rishonim, but the general pattern is as we have described.[50]

The Sage is Superior to the Prophet
The Talmud Yerushalmi (Avoda Zara 2:7) states:

> A Prophet and a Sage – to what may they be compared? To a king who sent two of his emissaries to the provinces. About one he wrote: "If he does not show you my seal and signet, do not

---

[49] Rabbi Moshe Shirken.
[50] See below "On the Shoulders of Giants" page 65 for another approach to cases of later authorities appearing superior to earlier ones.

believe him," and about the other he wrote: "Even though he does not show you my seal and signet, believe him." So too, regarding a Prophet, it is written: "And he shows you a sign or a wonder" (Devarim 13:2). But here [regarding a Sage]: "According to the instruction which they shall tell you" (Devarim 17:11).

"*Chacham adif mi navi* - the Sage is superior to the Prophet" (B. Batra 12a). Ramban explains that when prophecy passed to the Sages, prophecy now speaks "from within the Sage..." (Ramban is referring to the new level of perception of the Sages as a form of "prophecy;" this is clearly not prophecy in its classical form), there is an aspect of the wisdom of the Sages that is superior to prophecy. The Sages have the power to derive the truth from within their own consciousness, something that the prophets did not do. Indeed, the new "prophecy" that has become embedded in the Sages can paradoxically reach heights unattainable by the classical prophets - Rabbi Akiva and his colleagues were able to enter the *Pardes* ("Orchard") of kabbalistic worlds and effect changes there that no prophet could have done.[51] The prophets were superior in that they were addressed by God and shown visions from higher worlds; the Sages did not have those forms of revelation but they reached into even higher worlds from within their own minds.[52]

Carved in Stone
As noted, the Oral Law was *written* on the first Tablets (Bet Halevi Part 2, *drush* 18, quoting T. Yerushalmi). The meaning of this is that at the level of the first Tablets there was *only* a Written Law. The entire law was written - at that level there was no place for a debate to evolve clarity; all Torah had the explicit clarity of the Written Torah. All the myriad detailed applications and nuances of Torah were explicit and unmistakable. The second Tablets were entirely different - they were carved by human hand at a level far below that of the first Tablets, they transmitted only the roots of the Written Law; the Oral Law had begun its journey through history from mouth to mouth. Previously the whole perfect unity was carved in stone; now it must be transmitted and evolved in equal measure.

---

[51] Leshem Shvo V'Achlama, Sefer HaDeah Part 2, *anaf* 24, *siman* 11. For other relevant sections of Leshem, see Shaarei Leshem 333-382.

[52] Maharal, First Introduction to Gevurot Hashem.

The World Stands on Three Things
Among the first teachings of the Sages of the Great Assembly is: "The world stands on three things: on Torah, on service (prayer), and on acts of kindness." What are they telling us here that is new? Was it not formerly true that the world stood on these things? In fact that is precisely the point: formerly, the world *did not stand on these;* it stood on the word of God. The existence of the world and its conduct did not depend on human activities at root; its foundation was the Divine word. What is new is that the world now stands on these three things, no longer on the animating word of God alone but on the power of Torah, service and acts of kindness. It now stands on those three facets of human duty and action.

Formerly, prophets were the facilitators of miracle; they were the channel that brought the Divine word and action into the world. Now that channel is sealed and that voice is silent; the Sages have acquired that power. The world now stands on those who manifest these three things. The masters of Torah, prayer, and the practice of kindness are now masters of the world; now it stands on them.[53]

Ravens and Doves - Torah Forms Reality
Masters of Torah possess the ability to issue a ruling in Torah that becomes a reality. It is an error to think that a Torah ruling is merely an attempt to determine the halachic truth of a situation. It is far more: in a very deep way every *p'sak* (ruling in Torah) establishes a new truth. Torah is the causative energy of Creation, it preceded the world like genes precede conception. A decision in Torah is no less creative than an adjustment in the genetic material that determines how conception will occur. If Torah forms reality as the tool of creation in God's hand, when Torah passes to the hands of the Sages *they* wield the tool of creation. A ruling in Torah brings about a new reality; astonishing as it may be, when a competent Sage rules in Torah his ruling is not correct only because he has fathomed the reality of the halachic status of the issue in question - but rather *because he has caused it to be that way*. This verges on the miraculous: objects and situations must bend their nature to fit the ruling that governs their status. This power may stop short of bringing about a

---

[53] This is why the Sages were able to manipulate nature with ease; if the world stands on their actions, those actions are fundamental to the shape of reality. See below page 95.

clearly visible physical change; that may be going too far, particularly at our very late stage in the process of historical spiritual devolution, but in principle the world takes its shape from Torah as the body takes its shape from its genes, and if Torah assumes a particular form the world must follow suit.

The *gemara* (Sanhedrin 99b-100a) teaches this principle thus:

> Rabbi Yosef says: "[Some say] 'How do the Rabbis benefit us with all their Torah study? They study Torah and Mishna only for their own benefit.' " Abaye said to him: "One who questions the benefit provided by the Rabbis is in the category of one who distorts Torah, because [by doing so he denies the Torah itself, as] it is written: "If not for My covenant [Torah] day and night, I would not have set the laws of heaven and earth" (Jeremiah 33:25). [The Torah is responsible for maintaining the existence of the entire world; if its study would cease at any time of day or night the world would cease to exist (see page 156 below)]...
>
> There are some who say: "Of what use are the Rabbis to us? They have never permitted us the raven nor forbidden us the dove." Whenever a [possibly] unkosher item was brought before Rava, if he saw a reason to permit it, he would say to them: "See, I have permitted you the raven." If there were reason to forbid it, he would say: "See, I have forbidden you the dove."

Torah underlies all existence, and the specifics of Torah underlie the specifics of existence. When an item of indeterminate status receives a definitive Torah ruling, it *becomes* what the ruling states that it is. The misunderstanding of Torah that the *gemara* is referring to here is that things are what they are; when the Torah brands ravens as unkosher and doves as kosher, it is fixing their reality and no Rabbi can change that; all the Rabbi can do is state the obvious - the raven is unkosher and the dove is kosher. When a Rabbi rules on some object he is merely labelling it according to its innate nature. Who needs Rabbis like that? They add nothing beyond what the Torah has already defined. Rava responds by teaching the astounding notion that when he issues a ruling he is forming a reality: the object in question takes its halachic identity from his ruling.

In effect what he has done is the equivalent of making a raven kosher and a dove unkosher.[54]

This relates deeply to the Sages' ability to perform miracles.[55]

On The Shoulders of Giants[56]

Despite the decline of the generations, there can be advances. In fact it is obvious that advances have occurred in many fields. There are areas of Torah, too, where it may be claimed that advances have been made. At first glance this may appear to contradict our thesis of inexorable decline. But there is no contradiction - the reason for this is that smaller people can see further when they stand on the shoulders of taller ones.

Newton (in a letter to Robert Hook dated 5 February 1675) famously wrote: "If I have seen further it is by standing on the shoulders of Giants."

Newton was preceded by Shibbolei HaLeket (Rabbi Zedekiah ben Avraham Anav; late 13th Century) who quotes Talmudic sources concerning the greatness of the former generations, and then explains how he can disagree with earlier authorities - he says that he is like a dwarf compared to the earlier generations but he dares to disagree with them only because he stands on their shoulders.

Later commentaries have pointed out that with regard to revelation, earlier generations had an advantage because they were closer to the source of revelation, but with regard to empirical matters later generations have the advantage because they benefit from the work done by those who came before. Successive stages add strand to strand until finally the rope is long enough; earlier generations labor but may not reach water, until finally the later ones are able to drink.

---

[54] See: A. Tatz, Worldmask (Targum Press, 1995) for a fuller account of this theme.
[55] See page 95.
[56] For a detailed history of this aphorism including its appearance in Rabbinic literature see: Robert K. Merton, On the Shoulders of Giants (University of Chicago Press, 1993).

Whether the analogy is height and seeing to a distance or depth and reaching water, the point is true. It may take generations to dig a well - or complete a historic human project. The first generations may do most of the work (in fact there is often a prior stage of dreamers who begin the project in conception alone), and never reach their goal. But after all that thankless work a small excavation at the bottom of a dry well will discover water. Who made the breakthrough? Only the last; but it is obvious that the credit is due across the entire history of the project.

Most (probably all) breakthroughs in human intellectual and scientific progress, even the most brilliant, were preceded by many incremental steps that made the final spectacular result possible. Often a very lengthy series of advances (and failures - of no less importance) were necessary. The latest advances in science and technology that make it possible to plumb the oceans, dissect the atom and visit the planets are in fact very small additions to an edifice that has been centuries in the making.

And the heaviest lifting is done at the earliest stages. The first steps, with no previous work to lean on, are the most heroic. As the project moves over time the additions become smaller. Abraham began the most significant project in the history of the world essentially on his own. All who added later walk in his long shadow. The project reaches ever further as the participants become ever smaller. Dwarfs on the shoulders of giants indeed.

Shibbolei HaLeket was in turn taking the analogy from his teacher Rabbi Isaiah di Trani (the Younger; Isaiah ben Elisha, born around 1180). Shibbolei HaLeket reports his teacher's words:

> How can a man contradict the words of the early teachers whose hearts were as wide as a great hall? He answered with this tale that he heard from the gentile scholars: The philosophers asked their most learned colleague: "Do we not agree that the earlier generations were wiser than we? Yet we often contradict them and claim that we are correct. How is this possible?" The philosopher answered: "Who can see further, a dwarf or a giant? I say the giant - for his eyes are higher than the eyes of the dwarf. But if the dwarf were astride the neck of the giant, who would see further? I say the dwarf because now his eyes are higher than the eyes of the giant. Thus we are dwarfs astride the necks of giants because we have seen their wisdom and move beyond it.

From the strength of their wisdom we have become wise and can say all that we say, but we are not greater than they."

R. Zadok HaKohen also quotes the image of dwarfs on the shoulders of giants to describe the later generations, but adds a radical nuance: that in some way the later generations have *more profound* vision despite their lower situation:

> I heard from our holy teacher [the Izhbitzer] in the name of R. Bunim [of Pshischa] that even though intellectual abilities decline with each generation, deep understanding ("the point of life in the heart") expands and becomes purified through the exile (Pri Tzaddik 5, 39).

> It is known that when someone perceives clearly, the light of that Gate [of perception] opens to the world and is then open to all, for this is a principle that God has established for all the generations, even though they continually decline in ability. For once these lights are made available... by the great among the Sages of Israel... they remain open permanently. Therefore even though later generations are inferior they maintain this quality, as dwarfs on [the shoulders of giants]... and they themselves continue the process of opening new Gates. Even though they are greatly inferior, their insights are more profound, for they have passed through the Gates opened for the earlier generations (Resisei Layla pp13-14).

The changing level of the generations over history is not a simple downward line; the picture is more nuanced that that. It is true that the overall dimensions of the human form are shrinking, history is moving from its head to its feet; and yet within that decline advances are made, new insights are gained as new gates are opened.

Chapter 6

The Origins of Argument

A feature of the transition from Written to Oral Law is the development of *machloket,* argument and dissension within Torah. Through all the generations of the transmission of the Written Law there were no arguments, or more accurately, no essentially unresolvable arguments, in Torah. The Mishna too, was transmitted intact with perfect fidelity from generation to generation until shortly after the era of the Prophets.

Rambam (Introduction to the Mishna) states:

> When any two people of equal intellect and depth who have equal knowledge of the relevant fundamentals derive logical conclusions they will not differ in their opinions; and if they do, their disagreement will be minor, as we find with Hillel and Shammai who disagreed only on isolated laws.

Rambam explains that Torah transmission was perfect at first. Arguments that arose were only in details that had *not* been transmitted from Sinai. The tradition from Sinai was intact; both Written and Oral Laws were passed down perfectly at that stage of history. Even when arguments arose between Hillel and Shamai (very few - Hillel and Shamai disagreed on only three matters - see Shabbat 15a for discussion), both opinions are true to Torah; both can be derived from Torah. This is an expression of *"Elu v'elu divrei Elokim chayim* - Both these and those are the words of the Living God" (Eruvin 13b).

While prophecy was alive it could always resolve differences of opinion. Unresolvable argument was not possible in essence in the face of prophetic clarity. Later, when prophecy is no longer accessible, differences may never be resolved.[57]

Immediately following the Great Assembly lived Shimon HaTzaddik ("a remnant of the Great Assembly" who had seen prophets); no arguments arose in his generation. He was succeeded by Antigonos, who was followed by Rabbi Yosef ben Yoezer and Rabbi Yosef ben Yochanan. The first unresolved argument in the transmission of the Oral Law took place then: between Rabbi Yose ben Yoezer and Rabbi Yose ben Yochanan ("From the days of Moses until the death of Yosef ben Yoezer they learned Torah like Moses our teacher. From then on, they were not able to learn Torah like Moses our teacher..." - Temura 15b) only two generations after Shimon HaTzaddik witnessed prophecy's end. This single disagreement continued for three generations, until Hillel and Shammai who argued about three more things; in the subsequent generation the students of Hillel and Shammai argued about many things. In fact the Talmud is essentially a record of debate within Torah.

Rambam continues:

> [Concerning a later age, however] the Sages said: "From the time that the students of Shammai and Hillel - students who did not serve their teachers adequately - increased, argument multiplied among Israel." When the intellectual diligence of the students lessened and their logical faculties weakened relative to Hillel and Shammai, dissension arose among them in their perceptions concerning many things, because each one's analysis was based on his own [limited] intellect and the [limited] principles that he possessed.

---

[57] Any argument that did arise in the age of prophecy was resolved by reference to prophecy: the argument over King David's fitness to rule and indeed his legitimate place among the Jewish people was finally resolved by reference to a prophetic tradition: "Thus have I received from the Bet Din of Shmuel Haramati (the prophet Samuel)..." (Yevamot 77a).

During the phase of the Written Law, transmission of Torah was clear and there was essentially nothing to argue about; the work of transmission of Torah in those generations was to hear, to understand and pass on its teaching. Prophecy says the things themselves; it cannot be misunderstood. Words in the era of prophecy say exactly what their speaker means; as noted, in Hebrew the word for a "word" and for a "thing" is the same - *davar,* because every thing in the world is no more than a concrete version of the Divine word that creates it. When prophecy disappears, words become whatever the listener wants to hear and perfect communication becomes all but impossible.[58] In the era of the Written Law the meaning of things is carved in stone, fixed and clear. In the era of the Oral Law the meaning of things is as unstable as the changing nuances in the dynamic of conversations; there is no solid stone to be carved, only the shifting sands of personal perceptions.

The phases of transmission were these:

Beginning with the Sinai experience, the clear Divine words of prophecy were passed down as the Written Law, and the Mishna was passed down orally, both without error. That phase of clarity persisted until the end of the Great Assembly and for a very short time thereafter - immediately following the Great Assembly individuals transmitted Torah no longer at the level of prophecy, but no less faithfully and accurately. Beginning with Shimon HaTzaddik,[59] single individuals held all of Torah and passed it on with no loss of information.

Later, no individual could hold all of Torah, and the *zugot,* pairs, shared the task of transmission. Each pair together encompassed all of Torah, each member of the pair holding one half of Torah.[60]

---

[58] See page 107.

[59] "Shimon" means hearing; the clarity of prophetic vision (a prophet is a "seer") was no more (see page 115). The title *"tzaddik"* is also significant: in the deeper wisdom, *tzaddik* refers to the quality of *yesod,* the faculty of reproduction *(tzaddik yesod olam).* Shimon HaTzaddik represents the transition from "parent" to "child" in the flow of the generations. See above, page 58.

[60] Each pair represents the right (Nasi of the Sanhedrin) and left (Av Bet Din) sides or *chessed* and *din* aspects of Torah, held in separate vessels, as noted above.

At the time of Yosef ben Yoezer and Yosef ben Yochanan, argument crept in for the first time. However, despite the argument, the transmission was intact because both sides of an argument were still true to the original Torah at that level (see *Elu v'Elu,* page 73). In the tension between the positions of the argument, the whole was contained. This continued until Hillel and Shammai, where the phase of *"elu v'elu... - both sides are true"* in its pristine sense ended; after them it began to fade.

In the generation of the students of Hillel and Shammai, arguments arose that were no longer at the same level of perfect harmony of parts; fractures became possible within the transmission of Torah. This downward process continued during the Mishnaic phase, arguments multiplying as the transmission splintered into multiple streams. By the late Mishnaic era there was no longer any guarantee that the truth would be reconstructed accurately in every case from assembling the various points of view (because of the possible loss of information that the ongoing splintering threatened), and eventually, in the days of Rabbi Judah the Prince, the danger of a breakdown of transmission was real enough that Rabbi Judah found it necessary to take the unprecedented step of writing down the Oral Law.[61]

Three centuries later Ravina and Rav Ashi extended that process by writing down the Babylonian *gemara*.[62] The result is a Talmud that is no longer the original monolithic unity transmitted from Sinai but one constructed from opposing parts that mesh to form the multi-dimensional complex that is the Oral Law (and yet always loyal to the original Torah received at Sinai; all elements of the Oral Law were latent in that from the beginning).

---

[61] Rambam, Introduction to the Mishna. Rabbi Judah the Prince and his contemporaries wrote the Mishna in such a way that all essential information would be captured, and yet in a compressed style that ensured that the oral process would continue - as anyone who has engaged Talmud will know: without extreme effort and a reliance on an oral transmission the Mishna cannot be understood correctly.

[62] Again, Ravina and Rav Ashi adopted the same strategy - although the *gemara* is far more expansive than the Mishna, it is also compressed and cryptic enough to make an oral element in its transmission essential. In fact, as history progresses the increasing volume (and increasingly explicit style) of written commentaries over time is a sign of decline - each successive generation needs more explicit explanation.

Elu v'Elu... Both Sides are True

One of the unique aspects of this unity is that both sides of an argument in Torah are true, even when those sides are mutually exclusive. This is the meaning of *"Elu v'elu divrei Elokim chaim* - Both these and those are the words of the living God" (Eruvin 13b; and see Ritva there). This is true not only in the more philosophical areas of Torah, where each side of an argument brings out a different facet of the subject,[63] but even in the field of *halacha* (practical law). This is hard to understand: how can opposing views concerning the practical issues of *halacha* both be true? Surely if a thing is permitted it cannot also be forbidden? And what about arguments of fact: how can both sides be true when the debate concerns hard facts?

For example: the *gemara* (Shabbat 63b) debates how the *tzitz* (worn on the forehead of the High Priest) was designed - were its words written vertically or horizontally? This certainly appears to be a debate about a fact. Indeed, testimony is given that it was actually seen: the *tzitz* was preserved in Rome, and Rabbi Eliezer testified that he had seen it (Sukkah 5a), and described its design precisely. Strangely, that evidence did not seem to settle the question. Why not? What could be better evidence than the fact itself?

The key to understanding this issue is to realize that the debates in Talmud are not about fact, but about Torah. The Talmud is not a repository of medical, astronomical, geographical or other facts. Its debates are not about realia in the world *but about the Torah of those realia* - what does the Torah say about them? That is the question to be settled. A Talmudic debate is not about a fact, but rather about what is *"p'shat in pasuk"* - what the verse says about that fact. Even where a fact can clearly be demonstrated, that will not solve the problem at hand - the debate was not about the fact in the first place. Let the fact be whatever it is - the debate is about Torah, and only about Torah. Now the Torah is multifaceted and multipotential; its verses can be analysed to bring out multiple meanings, and all may be true. Of course, in the world of practical action the debate must be settled decisively - only one opinion

---

[63] Arguments in *hashkafa,* Torah philosophy or outlook, need not reflect mutually exclusive opinions: many points of view can be true, each adding a facet of insight to a rich and multiplex conceptual area. If there are arguments here they are more about subtleties of understanding and primacy between the various positions (Rabbi E. E. Dessler).

can be ruled into law. That will be done; *halacha* must be decided. But whatever the *halacha* will be in any particular case will not affect the validity of all the potential meanings that the relevant verses hold. Rabbi Eliezer may have seen the *tzitz* in Rome, but that did not settle the debate because the debate was not about the historical *tzitz,* it was about the *halachic tzitz* - not what form it took at a particular point in space and time but what the Torah says its form should be. In actual fact at any particular point in history it had one form, but the verses that describe it in Torah have two, and both are valid.[64]

The Talmudic process is not simply a search for the "correct" position and a rejection of false alternatives, a one-dimensional tracking of the truth among distracting falsehoods. It is also the much more subtle process of discerning among competent options. Since multiple positions in Talmud are true, the result is an expanded and enriched reality, not a constricted one. This richness is a product of the darkness in which the Oral Law must feel its way.[65]

---

[64] See Rabbi Yitzchak Hutner (Pachad Yitzchak, Iggerot U'Ktavim 30) for a fuller discussion of this principle and related issues.

[65] At Succot we commemorate the Clouds of Glory that surrounded us in the desert; these relate to the cloud that covered the Mishkan (Tabernacle) and indeed, the cloud that covered Mount Sinai at the giving of the Torah. Why are clouds the setting for revelation? Clouds are the proverbial agents of obscurity. The idea here is that to reveal the spiritual, the material must be covered, subdued. The context for Divine revelation is thick cloud; when the external world is hidden, the inner world can manifest (Rabbi Moshe Shapira). As the spiritual clouds dissipate through history and the material world hardens into the only vision we have, Torah must be wrought from that context.

Chapter 7

The Sealing of the Talmud

The relative darkness of the phase of the Oral Law may be the necessary context for its creativity. But in that darkness, new dangers lurk.

A particularly malign issue arises when the intrinsically human element in Talmud is misunderstood as a vulnerability to crude error. An elementary misunderstanding here has led to the deriding of the Sages of the Talmud as limited by their own psychological or social constrictions, or bound by the values or the science of their times. This is no less than a denial of the validity of the Oral Law itself.

The relevant principle to grasp is this: the sealing of the Talmud was a critical step in the descent of Torah over history.[66] Prior to that, the purity of the Oral Law's transmission and its power to reach unerring conclusions were intact. After that, the Divine oversight that guided the Sages was no longer manifest in the same way. But while it lasted, for the full period of the Talmud's development until its sealing, the Sages operated at a transcendent level. To see the Sages of the Mishna and *gemara* as merely human, vulnerable to human misjudgement in the same sense as later generations is a basic error.

---

[66] Rambam in Introduction to Mishne Torah states that later courts are free to disagree with earlier ones, but only *after* the sealing of the Babylonian Talmud. No later court may rule against the Talmud.

(Of course, "later generations" includes luminaries like Rashi and Rambam; one would be rash indeed to regard them as vulnerable to misjudgement in the same way as lesser authorities of more recent eras. And even those much later figures must be treated with the respect due to the Torah aristocracy of any age - anyone competent enough to engage the teachings of the Vilna Gaon will need no assurance on that. But the point remains: the closing of the Talmud was the closing of a world.)

Just as the Great Assembly sealed Tanach (Scripture) and thereby introduced a new era governed by new rules, and just as Rabbi Judah the Prince took the unprecedented step of committing the Mishna to writing because full and accurate oral transmission could no longer be assured, so too the last of the Amoraim Rav Ashi and Ravina wrote down and sealed the Talmud and began yet another era in the devolving voyage of Torah through history. The essential change at the sealing of the Talmud was from a world of Sages whose teaching is guaranteed by *ruach ha'kodesh* (Divine inspiration) to a world in which no such guarantee applies.

The *gemara* (Baba Metzia 86a and Rashi there) states:

> Rabbi Judah the Prince and Rabbi Natan are the end of the Mishna (the last Tannaim, editors of the Mishna). Rav Ashi and Ravina are *sof hora'a* (the end of authoritative teaching; the editing and sealing of the Talmud). And your mnemonic for this is: *"Ad avo el mikdashei El avina l'acharitam* - Until I come to the Sanctuary of God and understand their end" (Psalms 73:17). [The *"...ashei"* and *"avina"* elements are a hint to Rav Ashi and Ravina, and "their end" is a hint to their final closing of the Talmud.]

That was another categorical step down in history. Prophecy ended with the Great Assembly; Divine immanence in Talmudic transmission ended with the sealing of the Babylonian Talmud. That step down from the authority of the Tannaim and Amoraim to that of post-Talmudic Rabbis is critical; no later Rabbi can rule against the *gemara*.[67]

---

[67] Noda B'Yehuda (Even HaEzer Tinyana 79) responding to a question about the permissibility of a man marrying a woman whose father's name is the same as his own (a concern raised by Rabbi Yehuda HaChassid) states that since that concern is not mentioned in the *gemara*, there is no problem with such a marriage. "Those who come after the Talmud have no authority to disagree with the Talmud. Anyone who argues with... the Talmud is not part of the transmission. If we find those who do, they are... not intending to set a general

The Sages and Scientific Error

Elu v'elu divrei Elokim chayim in the strictest sense applies only until Hillel and Shammai (see above); the term is used more loosely after that. However, until *stimat haTalmud* - the sealing of the Talmud, all Oral Law transmission retains the quality of *ruach hakodesh*; this means that *no statement of the Sages can be wrong*. The words of the Sages form reality (see above); what they say is Torah, and Torah cannot be wrong. What they say *must* be true: even where they rule against an explicit opinion expressed by God Himself, their view stands - God ratifies theirs over His (see above).

What the Sages say is Torah; *they are Torah,* and they cannot be wrong. However, that is true only where the Sages make a pronouncement *relevant to halacha;* where they teach *aggada,* non-halachic material, they freely use the scientific notions of their time as analogies for spiritual matters with no regard to the scientific validity of those notions - they are simply using what comes to hand as good metaphor.[68]

An uncritical student who equates the Talmudic Sages' use of invalid science or wild superstition when illustrating philosophical or mystical material with their *halachic* pronouncements is guilty of a very crude and undiscerning reading of Talmud. There is no reason to use valid science when teaching a non-scientific subject; if an effective analogy is required it can be drawn from anywhere. Even a child's fantasy story will do; why not? In much the same way that secular literature draws on fables, mythology and folklore for its metaphors, the Sages used well-known or easily grasped images or stories to illustrate their abstruse or esoteric teachings.[69]

---

halachic principle but [are ruling] only for a particular case or a particular time... The general principle remains as the *gemara* says. Since Rabbi Yehuda HaChassid rules against cases in the *gemara* he [must have] intended specific cases only..."

[68] Rabbi Moshe Shapira.

[69] A critic who requires the Sages to take responsibility for the scientific truth of their metaphors and parables is suspect: he would certainly not raise that objection in any literary work - it is common in literature (and occasional even in science) to draw analogies from the fabulous and the fantastic. When a serious intellectual or scientific point is being made and its author uses a fanciful notion - say, a fairy tale that everyone knows - to convey his meaning, no-one in his right mind would critique that author by questioning the scientific validity of his fairy tale; that would be seriously to miss the point.

But that is out of the question when it comes to *halacha:* if an invalid grasp of a scientific issue were the basis for a *halachic* ruling, that ruling would be invalid. Where a *halacha* is based on science, that science is part of Torah. In such matters, if the science falls the Torah falls. In this area the validity of the science is crucial. Here, if the Sages could be wrong about their science, they could be wrong about their Torah. *Ruach ha'kodesh* - the spiritual connection that guided the Sages until the closing of the Talmud gave them insight into the realia of science, astronomy and biology that was as reliable as their *halachic* insight. Where the science is the basis of *halacha,* the two are so tightly bound that one who says the Sages were wrong about science is saying they were wrong about Torah.[70]

It is true that there are a handful of scientific assertions in Talmud that we do not understand today. These are very few; they can probably be counted on one hand. But to decide that the Sages were naively wrong or that they blindly accepted the science of their day as absolute truth is childish: firstly, the Sages must have been acutely aware that scientific theory changes radically over time; it always has - no serious scientist can ever be confident that all of science is known. Revolutions in understanding are part of the history of science; if there is any unchanging law of science it is probably just that: that current theory will almost certainly be overturned sooner or later.[71] And furthermore, there is something dishonest in demonstrating examples of scientific fact that the Sages appear to have misunderstood and using those to discredit those Sages across the board without mentioning the dozens of examples of scientific fact that they were *right* about - and often astoundingly so: how did they know, for example, that all fish that have scales have fins? (Niddah 51b). What human with no access to a higher source of wisdom could dare to make such a statement with no fear of contradiction? Even today the oceans yield secrets previously unknown; what expert over two thousand years ago could claim such knowledge based only on the natural science of his day?

---

[70] See M. Meiselman, Torah, Chazal and Science (Israel Bookshop Publications 2013) for an extended discussion of these issues.

[71] The Structure of Scientific Revolutions by Thomas Kuhn (1962) is perhaps the best known work on this; it introduced the now well-known term "paradigm shift" to describe the radical revisions of theory that science experiences perennially.

Indeed, this point is made in the Talmud itself: the *gemara* (Chullin 60b) asks how Moses could have written in the Torah that there are only four animals that have particular combinations of physical features (signs of *kashrut* - three that chew the cud but lack split hooves and one that has split hooves but does not chew the cud) unless he was recording Divinely given information. What sensible human would have committed himself to such an easily falsifiable claim? All that would be required to expose his ignorance would be the discovery of one species that breaks his rule; and in a world that was still largely unexplored that would have been at the very least a distinct possibility.

Examples abound in Talmud of an uncanny knowledge of the natural world - from geology to biology to astronomy, the Sages used their knowledge of the world to rule in *halacha*. Over the centuries they have been proven correct time and again. It is clear to any objective observer that the Sages had access to a higher source of information. Those who focus on the few cases of scientific statements in Talmud that appear mistaken to our modern eyes while ignoring the many cases that demonstrate the opposite must be suspected of some kind of bias at best.

As with all the previous steps from level to level over history it is essential to understand the meaning and the consequences of the closing of the Talmud, the critical distinction between the eras of *halachic* infallibility[72] and subsequent eras. What the Sages say is reality; after the closure of the Talmud, that rule no longer applies unconditionally; *ruach hakodesh* is now a far rarer commodity.

---

[72] *Halachic* infallibility: not human infallibility. Humans are always subject to flaws. Moses himself made errors; no human is above that. But the Torah of Moses remains perfect and immutable. The point regarding Talmud is that *ruach ha'kodesh* guided the Talmudic process and its conclusions until Rav Ashi and Ravina. To that point the process is Divinely ratified; later that is no longer the case at the same level.

IV:
New Modes of Being

Chapter 8

Breakaways and Reforms

The phase of *"elu v'elu"* in which contradictory opinions are true is followed by a much lower phase in the history of *machloket* (argument) where both sides are not necessarily true. Its origins, however, are earlier, immediately following the demise of prophecy.

Argument among the Sages expands Torah and gives us a creative hand in its development, but there is a dark side to that openness. Precisely because humans can argue in Torah, they can argue against it too. The nature of an Oral Law is that it contains an inalienable human element; human genius can and must be channelled into its formation. But human ego can enter an open debate; people can confuse their own agendas with those of Torah. These are the two sides of the coin of independence. A consequence of the Oral Law's independence from its anchor in the Written is that human distortion becomes possible. The greatness of the Oral Law is that it gives us the opportunity to express ourselves and that is its danger too.

Breakaways and Reforms
Immediately following the ending of prophecy, reforms and distortions began. In every generation pretenders arise that claim to be the real Judaism; none survive, but they cause immeasurable damage in the course of their rise and fall.

One generation after Shimon HaTzaddik, the first such illicit claim was made. Tzaddok and Beitus, two students of Antigonos, claimed that an element of the Oral Law's teaching is false.[73] As soon as there was no longer prophecy (nor even those who had seen prophets - like Shimon HaTzaddik) to negate any false claim, such claims arose; it took no longer than that. And the first distorted claim was precisely about an element of the Oral Law that is *entirely* oral: they claimed that there is no such thing as a World to Come. The idea of a World to Come (and resurrection in that world) is not mentioned in the Written Torah; the Oral Law derives that principle from between its lines. And precisely because it cannot be shown openly in the text of the Written Torah they were able to deny it. What is written has the authority of prophecy, that cannot be denied. But the Oral Law's interpretation of the Written is open; that can be denied with no fear of contradiction from a text.

Tzaddok and Beitus claimed that since the Torah does not mention the World to Come, that is evidence that there is no such future world. In fact, they had heard a lecture of their teacher Antigonos in which he stated: "Do not be like servants who serve the Master for a reward; rather be like servants who serve the Master for no reward" (Avot 1:3). Their distorted rendition of his teaching was: Do not be like servants who serve the Master for a reward *because there is no reward...* Within their teacher's message they heard an overtone that was not there; and because this particular point cannot be clarified from the original written source they were able to propagate this falsehood. A movement of dissenters arose from this who caused great suffering and damage over many years - the Tzeddukim (Sadducees), who continued refusing to accept anything that is not explicit in Torah.

In the next generation, that of Rabbi Yehoshua ben Perachya, misunderstandings of a master's teaching gave rise to another division and breakaway (and again, it began with misunderstanding of the master's teachings).[74] That process continues to this day; renegades and defectors construe Torah to fit with modernity or convenience or the political correctness of their age to create empty alternatives to genuine Torah.

---

[73] Avot 1:3 and Avot d'Rabbi Natan 5:2.

[74] Sanhedrin 107b, Sotah 47a in unabridged editions.

Open to Misunderstanding
Why does Torah not defend itself against these distortions? Why does it not state all its positions in unmistakable black and white? The fact is that an oral tradition cannot be insulated from misinterpretation; no matter what is written, a tradition that lives in the dynamic of human transmission, passing as it must through the hearts and minds of its exponents, must be open. The Oral Law is the throbbing heart of Torah; without it Torah would be set in cold stone and be forever static. But for another reason, defence is not necessary: for those who seek to understand genuinely the truth will be clear, and for those who insist on distortion no defence will be good enough.

A classic illustration of this principle is found in the Midrash (B. Rabba 8):

> When Moses was writing the Torah at God's dictation, he paused when God instructed him to write "Let Us make man." Moses objected: "If I write 'Us' (in the plural), people may misunderstand the principle of Your unity... That is surely too dangerous." God responded: "Moses, write. Let the one who wants to make an error come and err." And why indeed does God express Himself in the plural? To teach a point of *derech eretz* (refined behavior) - when one in authority makes a decision affecting his subordinates, he should consult them first: God consulted the angels before creating man ("Let Us make man" expresses the joint action of God and His angelic "advisors"). From this one learns good conduct in relationships and human management.

Now the obvious question is this: is that benefit worth its risk? Imagine that someone offers you a business investment. You ask what you stand to gain if your investment succeeds, and you are told that the potential profit is very small. You ask what you stand to lose if it fails, and you are told: "Everything you own." That is certainly not an investment any sensible person would make. In the case of our Midrash, that is exactly what seems to be happening: the potential gain of the Torah's expressing God in the plural is to teach a fine point of *derech eretz* or good conduct. The potential loss is mistaking the most fundamental principle of God's unity, which amounts to denial of the whole Torah. That disproportion of risk to benefit is extreme. Why would God take such a risk?

The answer is this: "Moses, write. Let the one who wants to make an error come and err." *The one who wants to make an error...* there is no defence against the one who *wants* to err; no matter what the Torah writes that individual will find a way to misunderstand. If God expresses Himself in the singular here, this person will point to Divine Names that have a plural form... There will be no shortages of opportunity for distortion. There is no defence against wilful misinterpretation of Torah. And therefore the Torah speaks its truth with no attempt to foil the devious. The smallest point of *derech eretz* is worth teaching despite the apparent risk because in fact there is no risk: only those who seek to distort will be misled and they are going to be misled anyway. For millennia Jews have been reading "Let Us make man" and never has any serious student of Torah imagined that God is more than one because of that phrase. The Torah does not defend itself against wilful misinterpreters - it speaks only to the sincere.[75]

---

[75] Heard from R. Simcha Wasserman, quoting his father R. Elchanan Wasserman who cited Rabbi Y.D. Soloveichik (Bet Halevi). See Kovetz Ma'amarim (Ohr Elchanan 5760 ed.) p124 and p130.

Chapter 9

End of Miracles

The Great Assembly ended not only the age of prophecy but also the age of miracles. The two go hand in hand; when prophecy ends miracles must end because these are two facets of the same mode (Rambam, Ralbag; see page 88). Prophecy is the explicit speech from a higher world heard in this world and miracles are the open hand of that Speaker manifest here. The closing of prophecy was also the end of revealed miracles; from the time that prophecy ended we have not experienced an open miracle.

Types of Miracle
There are two general classes of miracle: *nes nigleh,* revealed, and *nes nistar,* hidden miracles. A hidden miracle takes the form of an extremely improbable coincidence; the coming together of events so unlikely that a message is clearly being delivered. But no matter how unlikely, nothing impossible takes place. A sufficiently sceptical observer will be free to deny the significance of such events; no matter how astonishing, the events *could* just be coincidence.

A revealed miracle is entirely different. Here, something apparently impossible occurs - a law of nature is broken. This is not just a question of probabilities; in the case of a revealed miracle, what happens *could not* be coincidence or any other logically possible operation.

To illustrate: while out for a run, you accidentally run off the edge of a cliff. You grab onto a twig growing out of the cliff face and hang there desperately until finally you feel the twig snap. But it just so happens that someone is practising throwing ropes over the edges of cliffs that day, and you grab his rope and are pulled to safety. Now that would no doubt impress you as highly significant, but a firm sceptic would point out that such an event proves nothing... it *could have been* coincidence.

However, if you run off the edge of a cliff, grab a twig which finally snaps, and you *levitate up and float to safety,* you would have a decidedly different response. That has nothing to do with probability or coincidence; that is the suspension of a law of nature, something that we perceive to be impossible.[76]

Revealed miracles occurred during the era of prophecy, but not since. We may experience coincidences, and even wildly unlikely coincidences, but not abrogations of nature. That phase is over. In the post-prophetic age, we see only events that *could* be explained by natural causes. Prophecy and open miracles are tightly connected: open miracles occurred only in the presence of prophets (Ralbag, Milchamot Hashem). Indeed, the connection between the two is so close that a miracle can establish the validity of a prophet - Rambam rules that a claimant to prophecy can prove his status either by predicting the future or by performing an open miracle (Foundations of Torah 7:7). The ability to perform miracles is intrinsic to the prophetic state.

The scepticism of the modern world concerning the existence of open miracles is based on our lack of experience of such events. We do not experience open miracles and are taught to regard miraculous historical accounts as unreliable tales from a primitive age; but that is completely wrong from a Torah perspective since previous ages were spiritually *more* sophisticated. We do not experience that class of miracles because we are too low; after the Great Assembly the Divine hand of *hashgacha* (Providence) reaches down into our world as it always has, but now it operates invisibly, hidden behind the facade of natural law.

---

[76] In fact, even a law of nature is no more that a description of frequent repetition; laws of nature do not oblige natural phenomena, they simply describe their repeated patterns (see below, Science and Miracles, page 153 for discussion of this point). Despite that, however, we perceive abrogations of natural law very differently than coincidences that do not break natural law. That difference is enough to distinguish "hidden miracles" from "revealed miracles."

Miracle within Miracle - Revealing the Name

Revealed miracles themselves manifest on two levels: miracle *(nes)*, and a higher form, miracle within miracle *(nes b'toch nes)*. From Creation until the Exodus, revealed miracles took the form of supernatural events that temporarily set aside natural law - Abraham was cast into a furnace and survived, the barren Sarah conceived and gave birth at an impossibly old age, among others. From the period of the Exodus, however, a new and higher form of miracle was revealed: not by setting aside natural law, but by a complete negation of the laws of nature at root. When the waters of the Nile turned to blood, the water became blood for the Egyptians *while remaining water for the Jews*. The Midrash (Shmot Rabbah 9:10) states that if a Jew and an Egyptian drank from the same cup, the Jew drank water and the Egyptian drank blood. It is inaccurate to imagine that the substance was water in the cup but turned to blood in the mouth of the Egyptian. The miracle was far deeper than that: the correct understanding is that the substance was paradoxically water and blood at the same time, water for the Jews and blood for the Egyptians.

The source of this new class of miracle lies in the new revelation of the Divine Name that began to manifest with the events of the Exodus. God said to Moses (Shmot 6:3): "I appeared to the Fathers Abraham, Isaac and Jacob with my Name *Kel Shakai*..., but my Name of Essence I did not reveal to them." The Name of Essence, the Name that expresses God's timeless and creative Being, is the Name that transcends all logical limitations. It is the Name of the unity of all phenomena and unites paradoxical opposites.[77] That Name was not openly revealed to the Fathers; they knew it only at a distance. The Fathers experienced miracles (Abraham was cast into a fire and survived), but not miracles that obliterated nature entirely. After all, there are substances that can enter fire and not combust; flammable materials can be protected from flame. To be sure, it is miraculous when a human is cast into a fire and survives, but that form of miracle does not dissolve a law of nature at root. When water becomes blood and yet remains water simultaneously, however, something completely different has happened. That is the tangible manifestation of a logical impossibility. That is precisely the new level of immanence that was revealed by the Exodus. That process revealed to the nascent Jewish people a closeness to God not previously manifest directly

---

[77] This Name is the root of all paradoxical truths: *yedia* and *bechira* - Divine foreknowledge and free will, *rachamim* despite *din* - Divine mercy despite Divine justice (see below).

even to those great individuals who founded the Jewish people. (That would have to wait for the unity of individuals *in a nation* formed in the crucible of the Exodus.)

The culmination of that sequence of events was the giving of the Torah at Sinai. The miracles of those events took the form of paradoxical impossibility. The One God was revealing Himself, the unity of all that exists was becoming manifest, and ultimate oneness including the simultaneous existence of opposites was experienced.

Each of God's Names reveals a specific *middah* (spiritual quality). The Name of Essence is the name of the *middah* of *rachamim* (mercy). *Rachamim* is the *middah* that lies between *chessed* (kindness) on the right side and *din* (strict justice) on the left; it is the center and balance point between those two opposites. But this raises a question: how is the Name of Essence also the name of a single particular quality? The Name of Essence is the Name that expresses the totality of God as the Source of existence. The Name of Essence must express the totality of all the *middot,* not only one of them; how can it do both? How can it be the Name of all that is, and yet also be the Name of the one specific *middah* called *rachamim*?

The answer is that the essence of *rachamim* is that it combines opposites - it is the central point of unity that allows the contradictory qualities of *chessed* and *din* to co-exist (Ramchal, Klach Pitchei Chochma *ptach* 13). *Chessed* means kindness, the very opposite of strict justice which makes no allowances and no exceptions. Logically, these cannot possibly be combined - strict justice means no leniency; *chessed* means leniency. As soon as the leniency of *chessed* manifests, *din* disappears - these qualities are opposed by definition. And yet *rachamim* combines them - it allows the kindness of necessary leniency without mitigating justice in the least (Mesillat Yesharim, chapter 4). This is clearly a logical contradiction; and that is precisely what *rachamim* achieves - it bridges right and left without compromising either. *Rachamim* is not one isolated *middah;* it is the quality of unifying opposites, and that is why it is identified as the *middah* denoted by the Name of Essence of God. That Name is the expression of ultimate unity - even the unity of mutually exclusive opposites.

"Hear O Israel... God is One" does not mean only that there is one God and not two or more; that is a very basic message and should be obvious to anyone who thinks about it. "God is One" means not only that He is single *but that He is all that there is.* All existence is one with his; not only all things but also paradoxical opposites are united in His oneness. The quality of *rachamim* is the heart of all the *middot* - it is one *middah,* and yet it is the center at which all extremes melt into One.

The revelation of the Name at the Exodus was a revelation of the paradoxical unity of all existence, and it manifested in miracles that did not merely set nature aside but dissolved nature at root to show its underlying single Source. *Nes b'toch nes* - miracle within miracle.

At the Exodus the Jewish people came personally to know the God who generates the world's multiplicity and conflicting opposites and yet remains absolutely One.

The Tablets and the Torah were contained in the Ark. The *gemara* (Yoma 21a) states: "*Makom aron eino min ha'midda* - the space occupied by the Ark has no measure." The Ark occupied no space - a measurement from wall to wall of the Holy of Holies would have yielded the same dimension as a measurement from wall to Ark on both sides; it was a physical object that occupied no space. This is a negation of the dimension of space itself, not a temporary expansion or contraction - if the Ark had miraculously shrunk, or the Holy of Holies miraculously expanded, that would have been a miracle of the pre-Exodus type, "merely" a setting aside of natural law. But that could not have been the case: if the Ark had contracted it would have been invalid - the Ark has absolutely required specified dimensions. Similarly, if the Holy of Holies had expanded, it too would have been invalid for the same reason. Here, an object retained its spatial dimensions and yet occupied no space. (Here, in the Holy of Holies at the spiritual center of the universe, the conventional notion of space does not apply. This is where space itself comes into being. Here, the usual rules of space do not operate.[78]) That is

---

[78] Space emanates from that dimensionless point in concentric layers from the more intensely miraculous to the natural: in the Holy of Holies in the Temple the Ark occupies no space; in the courtyard of the Temple people stood crowded and yet were able to prostrate themselves in the same area with room to spare; in Jerusalem "no-one ever said he could not find a place to lodge;" and the land of Israel *("eretz tzvi")* "stretches" to absorb all her children "like the hide of a deer that (when skinned) appears too small to cover it...," and finally the rest of the world outside Israel where space behaves conventionally - descending levels of holiness as space moves outward from its point of origin.

a total negation of natural law, manifest openly in the world while utterly beyond human grasp.

When the ocean split to allow the Jewish people to cross, the Torah states that the Jews "walked on dry land in the midst of the ocean" (Shmot 14:22 and 14:29). A first reading may suggest that the Jews walked on dry land *where the ocean had been;* but that is not what the verse says - the words are: "on dry land in the midst of the ocean." Simply and accurately read this means that they walked on dry land *in the midst of the ocean* - it was dry land and ocean *at the same time* (see Sfat Emet, Pesach 5631, who says precisely that):

> It is written: "And the people of Israel entered the midst of the ocean on dry land" - the essence of the wonder was that they walked in the midst of the ocean literally, and [yet] it was dry land for them. For if it had been changed from being ocean that would not have been such a wonder; certainly God can change ocean to dry land. But from [His] love of Israel God made it literally ocean and despite that He made it dry land for Israel. The Jewish people are able to transform nature itself so that sanctity can literally be brought into it by their service [of God]. That is [the meaning of] "And he caused us to cross within it on dry land."

The Jews were born in a dimension beyond all natural law; that is intrinsic to the Exodus and the coming into being of a people who will transcend the laws of nature and history.

At the level of open miracle, God reveals that He controls nature; at the level of miracle within miracle, God reveals that He is all that there is. The revelation of the Name that demonstrates that level of connection with God was in fact the purpose of the Exodus.

This is the nature of the plagues in Egypt. The plague of hail consisted of hail that contained fire (Shmot 9:24; Shmot Rabba 12:4 comments: *"nes b'toch nes"*). This does not mean that large hailstones fell containing fire in their hollow centers. It means that the hail consisted of *fire and ice together;* both opposites manifesting fully and fiercely without negating or extinguishing each other in the least. The Exodus demonstrated God Himself in the world; not simply evidence of His existence by inference from the bending of natural law (though that is good enough evidence too!). Unlike the previous prophetic experience of the Fathers of the Jewish people, the Exodus brought into human experience the presence of God directly in the world; the Exodus gave birth to a people who would know that Presence personally and immediately, not simply know it by intellectual inference. The Sinai revelation was the culmination of that demonstration, a direct meeting of God and His people.

What was Revealed at Sinai?
Rambam (Foundations of Torah 8:1) writes that one who believes because of miracles and wonders has some imperfection in his faith:

> The Jewish people did not believe in Moses because of the miracles that he performed, for anyone who believes because of miracles has some imperfection in his heart, for it is possible for a miracle to be performed by means of sorcery... Rather, the miracles that were performed by Moses in the desert were done because they were necessary, not in order to prove his prophecy... Why indeed did they believe in him? Because of the Sinai experience, where our eyes saw and no stranger's; our ears heard and not another's...

A superficial reading of this Rambam suggests that miracles are unreliable evidence and that the Sinai revelation closed that gap - the miracles of the Exodus were not conclusive proof, but Sinai left no doubt; the personal experience of Sinai clinched the question of belief. But that cannot be the correct reading: after all, God Himself announced in Egypt that He would perform miracles to convince the Egyptians of His existence and power.[79] Evidently, miracles are good enough proof - God states clearly that He will send miracles as proof - and to the Egyptians, no less. The Egyptians were most unlikely to be convinced by dubious evidence - they were decidedly resistant to the idea of the Jewish God. If miracles are unreliable, why use them? And the fact is that the Egyptians got the message; though they were most certainly resistant to it to start with, they heard it loud and clear. So miracles are clearly adequate proof.

---

[79] Many verses make it clear that the miracles in Egypt were for the purpose of establishing God's existence and strength: "In order that the Egyptians will know that I am God" (Shmot 7:5; 14:18); "You will know that I am God when... the Nile turns to blood" (Shmot 7:17); "I will send all My plagues against you... so that you shall know that there is none like Me in all the earth" (Shmot 9:14).

But if that is the case, why did we need a Sinai revelation at which "our eyes saw... and our ears heard"? If miracles are good enough evidence, what was added at Sinai - why did we need that extra level of clarity? (And if miracles alone are not good enough, how would it be fair to expect the Egyptians to believe *without* a Sinai experience?)

The answer is that the miracles in Egypt were certainly proof enough of God's existence; the Torah states clearly that their purpose was indeed that. The miracles in Egypt were more than enough to demonstrate all that was necessary about God's existence and power. The Sinai experience was not to impress us with a better proof; we had all the proof we needed by then. Rather, Sinai was for *the experience of a direct meeting* between God and His people (that He should "kiss (us) with the kisses of His mouth" - Song of Songs 1:2). In the words of Rabbi Moshe Shapira: *"Ze lo inyan shel otzmat ha'hochacha - ze inyan shel eichut ha'yedia."* We did not go to Sinai for a more powerful proof; we went there for a *different kind of knowledge.*

We stood at Sinai for the intimacy of a marriage with God. The miracles in Egypt proved all that was needed, but miracles prove their point *by inference* - if nature can be overridden, that proves that God is in charge. The inference is strong, the proof is good; it works. But inference is not direct experience: one who believes by logical inference has an imperfection in his heart - *not* because he retains a degree of doubt, but because he lacks direct experience. Sinai was a direct, unmediated, intimate contact; that is why we went there. And *that is not for Egyptians.* That is for us; that meeting set the Jewish soul on fire forever. It began the Jewish path through history, and it burned fiercely enough to ensure Jewish attachment to God and His Torah through the torments of centuries.

Once in history there was an experience that transcended miracles. After that, miracles continued; first open and later hidden.

The Problem of Later Miracles
Revealed miracles ended during the era of the Great Assembly; between Purim and Chanuka, to be precise (see pages 131 and 163).

The *gemara* (Yoma 29a) states that there were no open miracles after Chanuka. This assertion, however, can be challenged from even a cursory study of Talmud. The Talmud documents revealed miracles occurring throughout its period of existence, long after the Great Assembly had passed from the world. This seems to be in clear contradiction to our principle. The Sages of the Talmud lived long after, and were far below, the level of the prophets and yet were able to produce miracles with apparent ease. How is this to be resolved with our principle?

Leshem Shvo V'Achlama deals with this question (Klallim, *klal 2 anaf* 3:1-10 especially 9). He points out that the miracles of Torah were few and far between, and each was highly significant - important enough to be part of the Torah itself. The miracles of the Talmud, on the other hand, were commonplace[80] and apparently not of major significance - they are often mentioned parenthetically, relevant to some point the Talmud is making but not of much importance in their own right.

Each miracle in Torah is a major event worthy of being enshrined in the written Torah - the splitting of the sea was a major upheaval worthy of forming part of Torah, as was the splitting of the Jordan; but in Talmud there is a case of a Tanna splitting a river with almost casual ease (see below, page 158). Abraham is thrown into a furnace and survives, as do Chananya, Mishael and Azarya, but the Talmud (Ketubot 67b) documents the case (long after all prophecy had ceased) of Mar Ukva and his wife entering a baker's oven (and surviving) for the purpose of avoiding embarrassing an individual (and the Talmud tells that story not to demonstrate their spiritual greatness but only to show that it is better to enter a fire than to cause embarrassment). Elijah revives the dead once, Elisha twice - these are rare and momentous events worthy of being recorded in Torah; however in Talmud these miracles are almost unremarkable.[81]

---

[80] Rabbi Chanina ben Dosa placed his foot over the lair of a poisonous serpent to teach that "serpents do not kill; only sin kills" (Brachot 33a). The serpent duly bit him - and it died. (Commentaries ask how Rabbi Chanina could have exposed himself to such danger - and answer that there was no danger at all. The only danger was to the serpent, not the Rabbi!) Rabbi Chanina's wife baked bread with no dough (Taanit 25a); Rabbi Zeira tested himself monthly by fire to assure himself that he was maintaining an appropriate level of sanctity (B. Metzia 85a)...

[81] Rabbi Chanina bar Chama, a student of Rabbi Judah the Prince, revived a dead slave whereupon the Roman Antoninus testified that he knew that even the most junior of Rabbi Judah's students was capable of such feats (Avoda Zara 10b).

And further, how can Rambam hold that the performance of a miracle establishes the credentials of a prophet (Foundations of Torah 7:7) - if we see that the Sages of the Mishna and *gemara* were able to produce miracles and it is clear beyond all doubt that they were nowhere near the level of prophecy, what proof of prophecy can be inferred from the performance of a miracle? Perhaps the miracle worker trying to establish his prophetic status is merely at the level of a Sage?

The answer is that on the contrary, it is precisely because the Sages are far below the level of prophets that they can control the natural. Because of the lack of Divine immanence these miracles can occur - because God has stepped back from His world, humans who are great enough in Torah can operate in a way previously impossible. Formerly, miracles were produced by God Himself, His direct presence in the world manifesting as miracle. The prophet was the channel; Divine immanence was revealed by the prophet's presence and by the miracle he facilitated. The miracle was proof of prophecy because no mere human could set aside the natural - God was in direct contact with His world and all that occurred in it represented His action. There was no place for humans to act independently in overriding nature. A miracle in that phase of history was a manifestation of God's presence in the world.

But later, when God stepped back and handed control of the world to the Sages of the Oral Law they gained the ability to move the natural in previously impossible ways not because they were prophets but *precisely because they were not*. Miracles now do not prove anything, and they are as commonplace as the Sages who perform them care to make them. And in this phase of history there is no question of using a miracle to prove prophecy - that level has long since disappeared and if a person produces a miracle now all that proves is that he is great enough to perform that miracle; *he* has that capacity, *he* is moving the natural world, not that God has entered directly into the world.

In Torah times a revealed miracle was no less than the appearance of the Divine in the material world, but in the phase of the Oral Law a "revealed miracle" is no more than a manipulation of the natural by human spiritual greatness. Once the phase of revealed miracles is closed, humans assume the mantle of action and control in the world and become able to move nature. When God steps behind the veil He hands over control of the physical universe to His Sages; Torah is no longer in Heaven, it is here among the Sages and its creative power is now in their hands. They create Torah, and they move the world.[82]

"The world stands on three things...." (Avot 1,2). The power to perform miracles now lies in the hands of those who represent the three pillars of the world: Torah, service (prayer) and acts of kindness. The masters of these are the masters of the world of physical phenomena. Each of the Sages recorded in the Talmud as the agent of a miracle was great in one of these areas.

Torah is the hands of the Sages; Torah creates and conditions reality, and the Sages who are now the definitive locus of Torah in the world have harnessed its power.

Leshem says this:

> [Despite the greatness of the earlier generations] it is a wonder of the Creator and His mysterious conduct of the world, intended from the beginning, to reveal His holy light and to give the keys of Creation and the secrets of the world only to the later generations, from the Second Temple period onwards. This treasure was given specifically to them, to have control over the order of Creation, until the end of the period of the founders of the Oral Law. They were given this precious gift to use as they wished, far more than to the early generations.
>
> As it states in Heichalot d'Rabbi Yishmael (27-29): Said Rabbi Yishmael: "Rabbi Akiva said in the name of Rabbi Eliezer the Great: Our fathers [of the Second Temple period] did not agree to begin building the Sanctuary until they prevailed upon the King of the world and all His hosts to reveal to them the secret[s] of the Torah... From the day that the Torah was given to Israel [at Sinai] until the Second Temple was built, Torah was given, but its glory, honor, greatness, awesomeness, richness, pride, uplifting genius, radiance... and might were not given until the Second Temple was built." And it further says that they were given permission to stand before the Throne of Glory as if they were sitting in the yeshiva, and they grasped the crown and

---

[82] See A. Tatz, Worldmask (Targum 1995) for extended discussion and examples.

received the seal and learned the secret Torah. [And God said to them] "From my storehouses and treasure chambers nothing is withheld from you - ask what you wish and it shall be given to you... I never intended to give [these treasures] to any of the generations from Moses until now; they have been saved for this generation to use, [from now] until the last generation." And about this it was said (Chaggai 2:9): "Greater will be the glory of the last House [the Second Temple] than the First."

Chapter 10

Blessings Composed

The Men of the Great Assembly composed the *brachot*, blessings, that we say today (and most of our liturgy: "The Men of the Great Assembly composed for Israel *brachot, tefillot, kedushot* and *havdalot*..." - Brachot 33a). Judaism without blessings is unthinkable - we pronounce blessings on virtually every human activity, pleasure and mitzva.

Before the time of the Great Assembly there were no formally obligatory blessings (with the exception of *bircat hamazon*, grace after meals, and the blessings on learning Torah, which are Torah obligations).[83] Jews lived without a *siddur* (prayerbook). Today we pronounce blessings on every aspect of Jewish life. Even the form of our prayers comprises blessings: the daily *amidah* consists of nineteen blessings, and it is introduced and followed by a series of blessings. Every food we enjoy has its particular mandated blessing, and sometimes more than one - blessings both precede and follow eating. Mitzvot are accompanied by blessings. It is hard to appreciate the extent of this change in Jewish

---

[83] There were blessings before the Great Assembly; indeed a verse posits the implied obligation to pronounce a hundred blessings daily (Menachot 43b). But no fixed text was prescribed; Jews expressed their blessings in individual and spontaneous manner. The Great Assembly composed and fixed specific blessings on virtually all of Jewish life.

practice - from life without formal blessings to life that is constantly accompanied by them. From waking in the morning to preparing for sleep at night, from youth to maturity, the events that form the cycle of life all move to the refrain of blessings.

Why were blessings unnecessary before the Great Assembly and universally necessary after them?

The key to this question is an understanding of the meaning of blessings. Nefesh HaChaim explains that a blessing is a pointed identification of Source. The meaning of *"Baruch Atah Hashem... Blessed are You, God..."* states Nefesh Hachaim, is "You, God, are the source of..." The expression of a blessing is an identification of the source of the thing on which that blessing is pronounced. The blessing explicitly acknowledges God as the source of the food about to be eaten or the mitzva about to be performed. *Baruch Atah Hashem Elokeinu melech haolam borei pri ha'eitz* means "You, God, are the source of the blessing which manifests as this fruit."

Before the Great Assembly, during the generations of prophecy, the world was illuminated, incandescent with its inner meaning. A world in which prophecy is available and miracles occur is a different world than the one we inhabit now. The world of prophecy does not obscure as the modern world does. A world in which prophecy lives does not mean only that individual prophets were to be found who could reveal the future and interpret the present clearly. A world in which prophecy is manifest is *generally* more illuminated. Even those who are not prophets in such a world see more clearly. When great luminaries shine in the world even the dark corners receive some of the glow.

In that world objects spoke their message clearly. Every *davar,* object, was a *davar,* word of God. *No effort of identification of Source was necessary because all things spoke clearly of their Source.*

In truth, every object in the world is nothing other than the word of God that creates it. As we have noted, in Hebrew, unlike other languages, both a "word" and a "thing" are expressed by the same word, *davar.* The world was created through speech: *"Vayomer Elokim* - And God said" does not mean that God issued an instruction, but much more deeply, that His pronouncement *became* the created object. The Divine statement "Let there be light" was the action of creating light - the word *"ohr"* condensed into the phenomenon of light. All things in the universe are none other than the words spoken to create them; every object in the world is the projection of a Divine word.[84]

Since objects are at root words, each object speaks its meaning. In essence the world was created as a dialogue; every thing in the world should speak its meaning clearly and simply by its existence alone. During the age of prophecy the world existed at a level where each object did indeed speak its word clearly - and there was no need to identify the source of any object. Each object spoke out its source; declaring that God is the source of an apple would have been superfluous, the apple itself said that. Now however, in the generations of darkness where nothing speaks clearly, it is necessary for us to identify the source of all things explicitly; therefore the men of the Great Assembly prescribed that exercise. The meaning of a blessing is exactly that - it is no more and no less than declaring the Source of an object that has fallen silent and no longer speaks for itself. In a world where every apple declares its Divine Source, blessings are unnecessary. In a world where an apple looks like an apple and no more, we must assert its Source. We must articulate the message of a dumb world.

---

[84] After the Flood, the world began again with the Word: the agency of survival that began the new phase of creation was Noah's Ark - the word for Ark is *tevah* - and *tevah* also means "word." (The dimensions of the Ark were 300 by 50 by 30 *amot;* the Hebrew letters corresponding to those three numbers are the letters of *lashon* - meaning "tongue" or "language".) See also Zohar, Noah; and Ramchal, Adir BaMarom.

Chapter 11

Prayers Composed

Beyond blessings - our prayers in general have a set form. Why did the Great Assembly find it necessary to compose a formal liturgy when that was not needed before? Why in fact do we pray this way - would it not be better to pray with spontaneous personal words? (Of course that is acceptable too; one may certainly add one's own personal prayers. The point here is why a set form of prayer is needed at all.)

A simple reason for set prayers is to articulate all that is necessary; spontaneous prayer may miss many essentials. A further reason is that the set prayers of the Great Assembly reach far beyond what any individual could currently compose or begin to articulate - the liturgy composed by the Great Assembly has unfathomable depth; that group of Sages and Prophets composed prayers that reach the heavens (Nefesh HaChaim 2:13), and that is good enough reason to say those prayers. But these reasons were apparently not enough to require the composition of a standard order of prayer before the time of the Great Assembly.

Rambam (Laws of Prayer 1:4) says this:

> During the exile in the days of Nebuchadnezzar, the Jews mingled with Persians, Greeks and other nations. In those foreign lands, children were born to them whose language was confused. Their language was a mixture of many languages; no-one was

able to express his thoughts adequately in any language. Therefore, when any of them prayed in Hebrew, he was unable to make his requests or praise God without mixing other languages with Hebrew. When Ezra and his Assembly realized this, they composed the *Shemoneh Esreh*... Their purpose was that the prayers should be in an organised form in everyone's mouth... For the same reason they composed all the blessings and prayers for all Jews so that every blessing should be familiar and current in the mouth of one who is not expert in speech.

In the time of Ezra during the Second Temple period it became apparent that direct communication with God had ended, as we have seen. The confusion of language that Rambam describes had deep roots; now that prophecy had ended there was no longer a channel for direct speech. The standardised prayer service was the response. Previously Jews indeed prayed spontaneously (Rambam, Laws of Prayer 1:2,3) in their own words at their own times. But that form of direct contact had ended; now we need a standard form to recite. When you are standing face to face with someone you do not read out a prepared statement, you simply speak. When the one you are addressing is distant, you may need to compose a message to send. When two communicate directly, face to face, they speak spontaneously. When the communication is at a distance, the conversation takes the form of messages sent between them. Formerly we spoke to God; now we recite a prepared composition to be forwarded. A face to face conversation has become a long distance exchange.[85]

Speech is an intimate connection. When the Mishna uses a euphemism for male-female intimacy, it chooses the metaphor of speech ("They saw her speaking to a man..." - Ketubot 13a). Speech connects; when the generation of Babel misused their speech for evil, they were dispersed as a consequence; permanently disconnected. In the prophetic era we heard God speak and we spoke to Him directly. In the post-prophetic era we must send our messages from a distance.

The Megilla of Esther describes a strange instruction sent out to the nations in the wake of Queen Vashti's death: "Let every man rule in his home and speak in the language of his nation." What is the meaning of this royal edict? The deep hint here is that as the world changes phase from one state of royalty to another (a change in the *midda* of *malchut*), a

---

[85] Rabbi Moshe Shapira.

new type of language is necessary; people must speak in a new way. Maharsha states that there is now a break between speaker and listener; people no longer really understand each other, and a new speech has become necessary. Esther's time in history is precisely the time that saw that change.[86]

Prayer was once a direct and immediate conversation. Now we send prepared messages. We no longer talk face to face with God in the way we once did, and we do not sense a direct response. That is the exile of communication that Rambam is referring to when he traces the origins of our modern form of prayer.

Reading the Signs
The distance that separates us also means that we can no longer reliably read the events of our lives as specific signs from a higher world. In the prophetic era the meaning of events could be discerned; a prophet could reveal their message. Now the messages are too veiled to read; life circumstances and events must be interpreted cautiously - just as we speak from a great distance, the replies we receive are correspondingly soft. Occasionally an event occurs whose meaning is so clear that it cannot be mistaken; that is a rare privilege. But most life events are not like that, and it is a mistake to read specific meaning into them. The meaning of events and the correct response to them must be decided with Torah wisdom and common sense; we do not have more direct tools. Much as we long to understand the details of the drama of life as it unfolds, our place in history makes that impossible.[87]

---

[86] See Purim, page 131.

[87] Rabbi Moshe Shapira.

Chapter 12

Change of Language

Language was originally the expression of essence. Words matched the world exactly. That is the nature of prophecy; it says the things themselves. The Creation began with language; at the deepest level a word is not simply a description of reality, it is an agent of Creation.[88]

The Zohar (2:161a/b) states:

> Meritorious is every one who strives in Torah... For the Holy One looked into the Torah and created the world, and with [by means of] Torah the world was created...
>
> The Torah preceded the world by two thousand years, and when the Holy One wished to create the world He looked into the Torah, at every word, and parallel [to each word] He crafted the world. Since all things and all events in all the worlds are in the Torah, the Holy One looked into it and created the world...

---

[88] Rashi (on Genesis 2:23, from B. Rabba 18:4) "This demonstrates that the world was created with *lashon hakodesh* - the holy language (Hebrew)..." The Midrash continues: "Just as the Torah was given in Hebrew, the world was created with Hebrew."

In Torah it is written: "In the beginning God created heaven and earth;" God looked at that word ["heaven"] and created heaven. In Torah it is written: "And God said 'Let there be light;' He looked at that word ["light"] and created light. And thus [He did] with every word that is written in Torah: He looked [at it] and made [that thing]... In this way the entire world was created.[89]

After the world was created each thing in it lacked [secure] existence, until He desired to create man, who would labor in Torah, and for him [by him] the world would be sustained. Now, anyone who looks into Torah and labors in it, as it were sustains the entire world. The Holy One looked into the Torah and created the world; a person looks into Torah and sustains the world. Thus the [source of] existence and maintenance of the entire world is Torah. Therefore meritorious is the person who strives in Torah, for he sustains the world.

Lashon hakodesh, the holy language, is the tool of creation. At the beginning of history the world spoke that language; communication was perfect at that level because in that language words do not talk *about* things, words *are* the things they express. A person speaking *lashon hakodesh* is presenting the things he is saying; he cannot be misunderstood. At the level of prophecy every *davar* (word) is precisely and tangibly the *davar* (object) it references. A prophet does not talk about a thing; he says the thing itself, and one who listens to a prophet does not hear a description of a thing, he experiences the thing itself.

The root *davar* means more than "word." In essence it means intelligent moving or placing or controlling - as in *"yadber amim tachtenu* - He will subdue nations under us"* (Psalms 47:4) or *"dabar echad l'dor* - there is one leader of a generation" (Sanhedrin 8a). In Aramaic *dabar* means moving or controlling, as in *"u'd'bar Hashem* - God took him" (God took Adam and placed him in the Garden - Genesis 2:15, Onkelos). *Dibbur* is more than merely speaking about things; in essence it is the

---

[89] Rabbi Moshe Shapira asked: why did God have to *look* into the Torah to create - surely He remembered what He had written? The answer is that the world is a copy of the Torah, and the *din* (law) is that when a *sofer* (scribe) copies a *sefer Torah* (Torah scroll) he is required to look at each word in the original before writing - he is forbidden to write from memory. Since God obeys His own laws, He looked before writing, to make the world a valid and perfect copy of the Torah.

root of action. Speech is the root of creation; it converts the abstract potential of thought into the reality of practical existence.

Speech connects the higher world of thought (the head) with the lower world of action (the body). The source of speech, the voice, is formed in the neck - that part of the human form that connects head and body.

The voice box is located in the front of the neck - the front of any structure represents its aspect of holiness, according to kabbalistic principles. The back of a structure represents the dark or fallen aspect. In kabbalistic thought the front of the neck is called "Moses" (*"Shechina medaberet mi'toch g'rono shel Moshe* - God speaks from Moses' throat"); the back of the neck is *"ha'oref"* in Hebrew. To see the dark side a word may be reversed; in this case, reversing the word *ha'oref* gives "Pharaoh." Moses represents the open speech of God in the world; the dark counterpoint to that is Pharaoh, the agent who blocks Divine expression.

In the body, the neck is the connector. In the world, the corresponding structure is the Temple. References to "the neck" in Torah are allusions to the Temple, as in the Song of Songs (4:4): *"K'migdal David tzavarech -* Like the tower of David is your neck," which is a reference to the Temple. When Joseph was reunited with Benjamin, the verse says: "And he fell upon the neck of Benjamin his brother and cried," on which Rashi (from B. Rabba 93:12) comments: "[He cried] for the Temples, which were to be in the territory of Benjamin, that would be ruined."

The Temple is the place of connection between worlds. From there, the word of God goes out.

Language and the Tower of Babel
Close to the beginning of human history there was a generation that plotted to use language to recreate the world in their own image - they built a tower to reach the Heavens and take control of the world.[90] Their tool was *lashon hakodesh* - they spoke *"safa achat u'devarim achadim,"*

---

[90] They attempted to build *"ir u'midgdal...* - a city and a tower whose top will reach the heavens" (Genesis 11:4). The "city" was to be Jerusalem and the "tower" was to be the Temple - but on the dark side, for the evil purpose of severing the world from its Source.

the single and unique language that has the power to create. They attempted to reconstitute the supernal persona of Adam by their total unity (they intended to recombine into an equivalent of the original supernal human who had the power to build or destroy the world) using the original language of Creation to control the world for their own nefarious purposes. And they could have done it - God Himself found it necessary to interfere. That interference took the form of confusing their language, breaking the tool they misused.[91]

The result was the breakdown of language in the world; from then, people do not speak the same language. This does not mean that the original Hebrew suddenly became Zulu and Chinese; that is a very superficial understanding indeed. The meaning is that the original *lashon hakodesh* in which all things had the unmistakable clarity of prophecy became the version of language that we have now: people speak *the same language* and no longer understand each other. Each hears not what is said but what he chooses to hear. Language has lost its holiness. Later, the process fractured further into the various languages of the nations and accurate translation is never possible,[92] but that is only a distant consequence of the original breakdown. In essence the problem is that perfect communication is now impossible. In fact, people generally understand each other in inverse proportion to the amount of talking that they need: two people who know each other well will understand each other clearly with only a hint or a gesture; that is all that is required. But when a lot of talking is necessary, the message is often more likely to be obscured than transmitted. As a general rule, the more you need to explain, the less chance you have of being understood.

That tower was built in Bavel, Babylon (Genesis 10:10; see Onkelos and Targum Yonatan). The breaking of language occurred there: "Let Us go down and confuse ('babble') their language." One man, Abraham, retained the original *lashon hakodesh*, the prophetic language, and went on to found a nation that spoke it. He transmitted it to his offspring, a nation that included more than a million prophets (Megilla 14a) over a

---

[91] The Ari (Likutei Torah, Noah) likens this to a king whose ministers had the keys to his treasure stores. When they began entering inappropriately, he changed the locks.

[92] See G. Steiner, After Babel (Oxford University Press 1975) on the problems of translation. (Italian captures the hopelessness of accurate translation with particular pithiness: "traduttore, traditore" - "the translator is a traitor.")

period of some thousand years - until the Babylonian exile. At that stage the Jewish people finally reached a point in the decline of history at which *lashon hakodesh* was no longer sustainable. That point coincided with an exile that sent us back to the place from which Abraham had come; back to the original crucible of his language.

The Reconstruction of Language

What was the Jewish people's response to that tragedy? Exiled to Bavel geographically and to the Bavel of language spiritually, we developed the Oral Law in the form of the Babylonian Talmud.[93] That Talmud is nothing less than a reconstruction of the holy language from its shards. When the vessel breaks and all that remains are its broken pieces there is only one solution: to reconstruct the vessel from the fragments. That is exactly the process of the Oral Law. The Talmudic method uses tentative and even wrong ideas *(hava aminos)* to reconstruct the truth. When all you have is fragments you must assemble those fragments to yield the whole. The Talmudic process is a unique reconstruction; unlike the conventional process of logical construction in which an axiom is laid down and complexity is layered upon that axiom, in Talmudic learning the starting assertion is typically wrong, but by demonstrating that, a better approximation to the truth emerges. That improved version is again shown to be inadequate, and a higher truth is revealed. So the process continues, essentially reconstructing truth from falsehood.

Resonating between the lines of the Babylonian Talmud, with its mixture of Hebrew and Aramaic and its handling of wrong ideas to extract right ones, is an echo of the original holy language.

Talmudic study is a training in deciphering a deceptive world. What appears at first glance is almost always wrong in the world's post-prophetic obscurity. Deep understanding requires paring away the illusion to reveal truth.

Spoken Language

Another change in language took place as a result of the Babylonian exile: the Jewish people stopped using Hebrew as their vernacular. Until that point Hebrew was used not only for Torah study and prayer, until

---

[93] The Jerusalem Talmud is written in a different style - see page 116 below.

First Temple times it served as the Jews' daily spoken medium. During the Second Temple period Jews chose to use other languages, even when they had to create them - Ladino or Yiddish, for example, and that has been the case until very recently. What was the reason for desisting from using Hebrew as an everyday language?

During prophetic times a holy language was appropriate for a holy life. At that high level everyday life had something of the holy, and Hebrew was the appropriate vessel for that. When consciousness is at a high enough level its language of expression retains its pristine nature. But when human consciousness falls to a level that is mundane at best and usually far worse, language becomes the tool of secular minds in an unsanctified world. At that point there is a real danger of the language becoming contaminated by the secular; its meanings will be secular and profane because that has become the mode of its speakers. When that happens it will be impossible to regain the higher mode: when the means are damaged the end will not be reached. When Hebrew falls to a secular level the higher concepts of Torah can be taught only with great difficulty: when high ideas are spoken in a language that has come to hold only the very limited meanings of a secular culture, those concepts are lost, and there is no medium for regaining them - the more the language attempts to describe them the more entrenched will their illusory substitutes become.

One has only to examine English to see this clearly: words like "Heaven," "Hell," "Satan," "angel" and "saint," let alone words for the Divine, evoke images from Renaissance paintings long before the rarefied abstractions that are intended. Languages express their cultures; religious words in the English language express the religious ideas of its host culture and there is no escaping that.[94]

Faced with the prospect of damaging the medium of holiness, it was set aside for holy use. Rather than allowing its words to descend into the constricted meanings of the secular and to lose its transcendent overtones, the Jewish people's sensitivity led them to other languages. In Jewish

---

[94] Teaching Torah to English-speaking newcomers is a real problem: in a language that distorts spiritual subtlety into the icons of Western religion, it is very difficult to open a new consciousness. The solution is to use the Torah terms for those ideas - bypassing the invalid perceptions that their language awakens.

communities throughout the world Hebrew became the language of Torah and prayer, and other languages were chosen for everyday use, not simply because the language of exile is more conveniently the spoken language of the host country; but for a far deeper reason.

Language takes on the meaning that we construct with it; every language is an expression of the culture that speaks it. A Torah culture requires a Torah language.

Chapter 13

From Seeing to Hearing

Language is heard, not seen. The transition from prophecy to Oral Law was a transition from the mode of seeing to the mode of hearing.

The two higher modes of human perception are seeing and hearing. Seeing is the higher of these, hearing the lower. Seeing takes place in the light; it grasps the entirety of a scene at once. Evidence can be given in Bet Din (Jewish court of law) in serious matters only when the witness has seen the relevant events.

Hearing is not like that. Hearing is a process of construction of parts: when speech is heard, it comprises a sequence of one syllable after another, and only when the last has been spoken does the meaning become apparent. Hearing is subjective; the listener must assemble the sounds of the sequence internally. More than one sound cannot be heard together; if that happens what is heard is simply noise.[95] The components of a picture are seen together and their integration is grasped at once; the components of an aural story must be connected by the listener.

Witnessed evidence is valid; hearsay is not.

---

[95] "Two sounds cannot be heard (discerned) at once" (R. Hashana 27a).

The word for hearing is *shema* - this root means "assembly," as in "*Vayeshama Shaul et ha'am* - And Saul gathered the people" (Samuel 1, 15:4). The statement *Shema Yisrael, Hashem Elokeinu, Hashem echad,* usually translated as "Hear O Israel..." is in fact an instruction to forge that oneness in the mind. *Shema* here is not simply a command to listen, but to assemble in consciousness all elements of the world, to make all one.

Seeing was the mode of the prophetic world; a prophet is called a "seer" *(chozeh)*. Hearing is the mode of the post-prophetic world; at our stage of history we do not see, we must strain our ears to hear in the darkness.

> Until that time [of Alexander of Macedon] the prophets prophesied through the Holy Spirit, from then on bend your ear and hear the words of the Sages (Seder Olam 30).

It is significant that when the Jerusalem Talmud and the Zohar, those documents that retain some connection to the world of clarity, wish to demonstrate a process they begin with *"ta chazi* – come and see." When the Babylonian Talmud, that exercise in reconstruction in darkness, begins an equivalent section, it begins *"ta shema* – come and hear." When clear-sighted perception breaks down we move to the phase of hearing, the phase of subjective construction.

This explains a perplexing statement in Torah describing the experience of the giving of the Torah at Sinai - the Torah states that the people "saw the sounds" that accompanied that event. In what way are sounds seen? Why is it necessary for the Torah to say this? The answer is that hearing is the relevant mode of perception only where a process is taking place; when a story is unfolding it can be heard. But when a static scene is being grasped it cannot be heard, it can only be seen. At Sinai, no story was in process: all of reality was manifest simultaneously - the Midrash (Shmot Rabba 29) states that when the Torah was given, nothing moved ("no bird chirped, no fowl flew...") The reason is that all things were at their point of destination then, no movement was required or even possible at that moment; all was perfectly in place, any movement could only have been away from essence. At such a moment, only seeing is possible. Hearing is the mode of subjective assembly; that is not relevant when objective reality manifests. Seeing is the mode of the Written Law; hearing is the mode of the Oral Law.

The Oral Law is grasped through a process of sensitive listening, by carefully hearing what its Sages have to say. The Written Torah, that book that was once the equivalent of "*v'nagolu k'sefer hashamayim -* And I will roll up the Heavens like a book" (Isaiah 34:4) is now the *sefer* (book) of the Oral Law, a carefully constructed *sippur* (story) of details none of which makes sense in itself but in the reconstructed telling gives a glimpse of what was once seen clearly.

Chapter 14

The New Beauty

Ramchal writes (Path of the Just, Introduction) that in the obscurity of night when vision has faded, two types of error are possible. One is the failure to see an object that exists. The other, more subtle, is to mistake one object for another; one sees, but perceives wrongly. In the darkness of the post-prophetic world one area of misperception is that of beauty, and particularly women's beauty

Torah makes much of its women's beauty - Eve, Sarah, Rachav, Avigail and others are presented as beautiful. Sarah, wife of Abraham, was exquisitely beautiful; her beauty was an echo of the beauty of Eve, the origin of all womanly beauty (B. Batra 58a). When the Torah presents Sarah's beauty it clearly means a sensual beauty, not some kind of spiritual aura - we can be sure of that because the Egyptians were ready to kill for her, and the Egyptians were certainly not seeking the spiritual; Egypt was the most depraved place on earth. She must have been ravishingly beautiful to Egyptian eyes.

Now why would the Torah tell us that? The Torah is a system of instruction for life and how to elevate it; why is it necessary to tell us that Sarah was beautiful? What does Sarah's beauty add to her righteousness, surely her essential quality? And not only woman - Joseph is described as beautiful; women climbed walls to get a glimpse of him (Genesis 49:22;

Rashi; R. Bachya). Why is his beauty important? This is even harder to understand than the relevance of feminine beauty.

It is clear that Torah portrays beauty as an aspect of essence. The Talmud goes so far as to state: *"Ein isha ela l'yofi... -* A wife is for beauty..." (Ketubot 59b). This is surprising, to say the least. But more perplexing is this: the Torah itself indicates that beauty is problematic. In praising its "Woman of Valor," Torah states explicitly that beauty is false and empty. King Solomon puts it thus: *"Sheker ha'chen v'hevel ha'yofi -* Charm is a lie and beauty is empty." Later, the Mishna states: *"Al tistakel b'kankan ela b'ma she'yesh bo* - Do not look at the vessel but at its contents" (Avot 4:27). From these sources it is evident that external beauty is irrelevant at best.

The definitive Talmudic teaching on this subject (Nedarim 50b) makes it clear that beauty is a problem. The *gemara* records a conversation between Rabbi Yehoshua ben Chananya, the *"chakima d'Yehudai -* the wise man of the Jews," and the Roman emperor's daughter. Apart from his greatness in Torah, Rabbi Chananya's outstanding feature was his ugliness. He was so strikingly ugly in fact, that she was moved to ask him: "How can such beautiful Torah be contained in such an ugly vessel?"

(It is not insignificant that the question was asked by a Roman woman. Rome was the cultural and intellectual legacy of Greece, and at the center of that legacy was the idea of esthetics. Beautiful content demands a beautiful container - that is the essence of the esthetics of art. The Greek games were played naked - "a healthy mind in a healthy body" was the ideal. Content is revealed in its mode of expression; the mode must be perfectly appropriate. It is woman who represents the expression of beauty, and she, a Roman woman, was unable to reconcile great wisdom contained in the vessel of a misshapen body.)

> She asked: "How can such beautiful Torah be contained in such an ugly vessel?"
>
> He replied: "Learn [the answer to your question] from your father's house. In what vessels do you keep your wine?"
>
> "In earthenware vessels," she answered. [The Emperor stored his wine in earthenware jars like everyone else.]

He said to her: "Everyone else [stores their wine] in earthenware vessels and you also store your wine in earthenware vessels? ["Is that fitting for royalty?] Surely you should put your wine into silver and gold vessels!"

[She agreed.] She returned to the palace and had her father's wine transferred to silver and gold vessels. [Of course, the alcohol in the wine reacted with the metal and] the wine soured.

Rabbi Yehoshua said to her: "The same is true of Torah [it is damaged when it is contained in a handsome person."]

A simple vessel holds its contents without adulteration; a vessel that asserts its own importance conflicts with its contents. Good looks may conflict with spiritual wisdom. A good looking body is likely to obstruct inner wisdom; a broken exterior will not.

Rabbi Yehoshua taught her that in the world of spiritual values, vessel and content are locked in mortal battle. The container must be simple for the contents to be pure. When the vessel is humble it does not detract from what it holds - Moses was the greatest man who ever lived, the vessel that contained the entire Torah, because he was the most humble. One who holds Torah must have no ego; any statement of the self will obstruct the projection of its contents. One who would project God into the world must be transparent. Body and soul are enemies; any assertion of the body is a defeat of the soul. If the body is beautiful, the wisdom it holds must be compromised.

However, the *gemara* records that the conversation did not end there. The Emperor's daughter was not convinced by Rabbi Yehoshua's answer.

["What about your colleagues?"] she asked, "There are Sages who are handsome *and* learned?"

(There were Sages who were extremely handsome - Rabbi Yishmael's beauty was legendary. Generations later, Rabbi Yochanan would visit a friend who was ill and due to his poverty lay in darkness; Rabbi Yochanan rolled up his sleeve and illuminated the house with the incandescence of his beauty (Brachot 5b). So she was perplexed: if ugliness is a prerequisite for wisdom, why are some Sages beautiful and wise?)

Rabbi Yehoshua answered: "Had they been ugly, they would have been wiser."

Those handsome Rabbis achieved wisdom despite the disadvantage of good looks. Certainly it can be done; wisdom can be acquired even by the handsome - but it is more difficult. To hold pure content, the vessel must add absolutely nothing. It must be utterly simple. A vessel with no pretensions of its own allows its contents to shine unobstructed. The vessel contains perfectly when it only contains. The ideal vessel is unnoticed. The ideal teacher is transparent - he demonstrates his subject, not himself. A good actor projects the part, not himself. A good medium delivers only its message.

Here we have a clear teaching on the nature of beauty: it is dangerous, obstructive. External beauty threatens inner content. In proportion to the beauty of the vessel the contents will be damaged.

So there is a sharp contrast within Torah on this subject: on the one hand Torah presents its great women (and Joseph) as beautiful, clearly as an aspect of their essence. And on the other, Torah teaches that beauty is in conflict with essence. Why does the same Torah that extols its great women's beauty also denigrate beauty in the clearest terms?

What is the resolution of this issue? Should vessels be beautiful to enhance their content or should they be ugly in order not to conflict with their content? Does a beautiful painting deserve a beautiful frame, or will it be shown to greater advantage by the simplest of frames? What is the ideal setting for a diamond? Should woman's beauty be projected or suppressed? What is the meaning of the Torah's equivocation here?

Once again, our key will unlock this mystery. In the first phase of history, external beauty was no enemy of inner content; when all aspects of the world revealed, outer structures revealed their inner content. In the second phase, when outer structures purport to be all that there is, inner content has very little chance of shining through. In this phase, only the simplest and most unassuming vessels are appropriate. Any assertion of the outer will pervert content.

An examination of the history of this problem will make this clearer. The battle between soul and body began with the first humans. Adam was created so that his light shone through his vessel so clearly that the light was almost all that was visible. Originally, Adam was literally a cosmic figure - he spanned the universe (Genesis Rabba 8); the light that shone from his heels after death was greater than the sun (B. Batra 58a). He was luminous; his soul shone so powerfully that his body was hardly discernible. He appeared as the converse of the current human form - now a human appears all body and the soul is all but invisible. The face may project a faint glow *(ziv ha'panim),* particularly in the case of one who is refined, who has invested a lifetime in spiritual effort (Moses' face shone so powerfully that he was obliged wear a veil - in this, he manifested the original beauty of Adam). There is no shame in the exposed face (and that is why there are no garments for the face). But this glow is very faint indeed, usually no more than a suggestion. When Adam was created he appeared precisely the opposite - his soul was entirely dominant and that is what was seen; close inspection might have revealed the wispy outlines of a body (Rabbi E. Dessler). Staring at a powerful electric light bulb will show only the light; it will take extreme effort to reveal the outline of the glass.

Adam and Eve inhabited bodies that were perfect vessels for their inner light; their bodies projected that light without obstructing it. That is why they did not need clothes. We are ashamed when we are naked because we experience the painful schism between an angelic inner being and an animal outer being. The human body is given to contamination and disintegration, contains its own excrement, in essence is animal. The tension between an elevated soul and the animal body that houses it generates the sense of shame.

Shame is the result of incommensurate states. When the inner potential for good is betrayed by external behavior that is bad, shame is generated. We are ashamed by our actions when they do not live up to our genuine values. We are ashamed when we do less, or worse, than we should have done. Shame is an expression of the discrepancy between potential and performance. One shames a person by showing them how their behavior is incompatible with their own standard (in fact that is the mitzva of *tochacha* - the obligation of reproof or rebuke consists of bringing a person to see their own inconsistency).

When Adam sinned he crashed his ethereal, transparent body into an earthy shell. The transparent skin through which a luminous soul had shone became the thick and opaque hide that it is now (B. Rabba 20:12). That is why he became ashamed.

When Adam was created he was virtually all spirit; his first-person "I" was only *neshamah*, soul. His animalistic aspect was the serpent at a distance addressing him as "You" in the second-person, entirely separate from his experience of self. The "I," his inner consciousness, was only spirit, and the distant, external, second-person "You" represented the sensual. His sin drew the sensuous, animal dimension into his being. After the sin, the body speaks in the first person. Now, when we say "I" we mean the body, the *yetzer hara* (the evil inclination) - the material, the lazy, the earthy. Consciousness now speaks from that self. This is clear - when you are tempted sensually, for example faced with something delicious that you would like to taste, which voice speaks? "I would like to taste that..." *I* would like. And the conscience - how does that speak? "You know you shouldn't..." *You* shouldn't. Our central sense of self has shifted.

Our bodies address us in the first person; our conscience in the second. That is the fall of man. We have become the opposite of our original pure selves; there has been a reversal of roles. The external sensual was a very distant voice, separate from the real self; now the "I" has become identified with the body, and the conscience, if it speaks at all, speaks from a distance. Now, the external dominates. The *gemara* (Succah 52b) states that the *yetzer* is first like a passer-by in the street, then like a beggar at the door, and finally rules as master of the house.

The human enterprise has been captured by the external. The spirit no longer dominates; the lower self has taken over. The lower self is called *tzfoni,* "the hidden one" (Succah 52a). There is no better way of hiding a thing than putting it in full view: no-one thinks of looking there. The *yetzer* is so skilfully hidden that it cannot be found because it is now consciousness itself, masquerading as the one doing the searching.

When Adam was all spirit the vessel of his body was totally loyal. The body projected the *neshamah* so perfectly it needed no clothes; nothing could have been more pointless than clothes. But after the crash the solution became clothing. When Adam sinned and felt his shame he initially tried to cover only the most shameful aspect of his body, and God responded by giving him a full set of clothes. The message is that clothes must not only hide nakedness but also reveal dignity. God sewed him garments of dignity (Genesis 3:21). Before Adam sinned he was clothed in garments of light, *ohr,* spelled with an *aleph;* after he sinned he became clothed in garments of *ohr* spelled with an *ayin* (B. Rabba 20:12;

Zohar, Genesis 1:36b). *Ohr* (*aleph*) means light; *ohr* (*ayin*) means skin. But *ohr* (*ayin*) also means "blind" (the same word read as *"iver"*). First he was clothed in light that revealed; now we are clothed in skin that hides - in fact "hide" means skin, a direct parallel of the Hebrew.

Now the inner can no longer be seen, only the animal is visible; that is our problem. The solution is garments. When a king wears royal garments they hide the king, but they reveal his royalty. The *gemara* states that Rabbi Yochanan referred to his clothes as "My dignity" (Shabbat 113a).

Of course, garments may hide too much. The word *beged* means "garment" and also "treachery." *Boged* is a traitor. (An outer garment is a *me'il*, coat, which also means treachery - *me'ila* means to betray the sanctity of the holy by using it for the profane.) Another word for a traitor is a "turncoat." That is the trade-off in this solution: hiding the body rescues its dignity, but the price is a false front. No longer can the raw truth be directly manifest; no longer can original beauty be allowed to shine. It has become too dangerously misleading.

When Adam and Eve's bodies revealed their soul, they knew no shame. When they cast the world into its present disparity where the body speaks only for itself, covering the body preserves its dignity - and that is the meaning of *tzniut,* or modesty.

As the darkness of history grows thicker, as the body becomes progressively more opaque, the problem worsens. There was a watershed moment in history when the darkness became so intense that from that time on, even the most elevated spiritual figures can no longer make the material shine.

That break point in history was Purim. That is when the transition took place: until then the world held enough light for great people to reveal the spiritual through the physical. Until then a woman's beauty could be a vehicle for revealing the spirit; from that time on it became all but impossible.

In this, Esther was the transitional personality; she teaches this principle. "Esther" means "the hidden one" - the *gemara* finds her name in Torah in the verse *"Hastir astir panai* - [On that day] I shall Hide My face" (Chullin 139b). The *gemara* (Megilla 15a) presents two opinions concerning her beauty. One view is that she was one of the four most beautiful women who ever lived. The other is that she was not good looking at all - in fact "she had a green face." Previously the Torah's great women were exceptionally beautiful; now we have a woman whose beauty is debatable. Both sides must be true (as with all arguments of this type in Torah). What is the meaning of this debate; what is the truth on both sides?

Purim straddles the divide of history.[96] On the one hand it manifests a miracle; it continues the phase of the revealed. That aspect gives Esther the transcendent beauty of the Matriarchs. But Purim ushers in the second phase of history, when miracles will be only of the hidden type. In this phase that original beauty can no longer manifest. Esther must be plain, at best. If she is to entice the Persian king it must be through a mysterious inner charm (*"chut shel chesed"*), not overt beauty. From now, external beauty will hide inner charm and betray it, not reveal it.

"*Hastir astir panai...* On that day I shall hide my face..." That day in Jewish history has arrived, and the woman who will save the Jewish people must manifest a new sort of beauty. Ironically, if there ever was a woman who needed beauty it was Esther - her role was to seize the king's attention; and yet God did not give her the conventional beauty that might be expected. She must do her work in the world without those good looks - but understood more deeply, *because* she does not possess them; hers is a deeper beauty, a beauty that must shine from within because if it manifests in conventional external form it will show only the external, and there is no charm in that in a fallen world.

There is a Midrash (Genesis Rabba 39:13) that states that she was seventy five years old at the time she was taken to become the queen. The girls that the Persian king assembled from across his kingdom must have been exquisitely beautiful. And competing for the king's attention among those beauties is a (married) Jewish woman who is much older, with a green face... This is clearly a different sort of beauty.

Esther lived at the junction between phases; the argument about her beauty reflects her position on the cusp of history. One view is that she had some of Eve's original beauty - like Sarah, she was able to reveal the spiritual through the material. The other is that she was a daughter of the

---

[96] See Purim, page 131.

second phase - no longer could her body shine transparently; like all those who lived after her she could reveal an inner charm only by tight control of the external.

In the earlier generations when the point of origin was clear, the body could not have been more beautiful; the praise of the body was the praise of the soul. At that time beautiful content needed beautiful vessels. But as we move down through history we reach the level where Rabbi Yehoshua ben Chananya lives and beauty is no longer an asset; it has become too dangerous. Now the painting needs the simplest of frames; any attention to the frame will only distract.

Womanly beauty was formerly an asset, it spoke truly; now it has been tainted by a world of falsehood - "*Sheker ha'chen v'hevel ha'yofi* - Charm is a lie and beauty is empty."[97]

Before that transition the greatest men in Jewish history reached back to a glimmer of Adam's beauty: Moses' face shone; he had to wear a veil to protect others from that intensity. The great women of Jewish history manifested some of Eve's original beauty: one of Sarah's names was Yiskah - the root of "Yiskah" is *socheh,* to see through. The *gemara* (Megilla 14a) says "*Ki hakol sochin b'yof'ya* - because everyone could see through her beauty." There are many Hebrew words for seeing - *roeh*, to see, *tzofeh*, to see from afar, *mabit*, to gaze, *mistakel*, to look, *shur*, to view. *Socheh* means to see through.[98] What does seeing through a woman's beauty mean?

Womanly beauty can be presented so that it brings the gaze down - sensual beauty can very easily be projected so that it suggests the animal. But it can also be presented in such a profound and refined way that it evokes the angelic. That is *tzniut*. The modesty of *tzniut* does not require invisibility or distortion. Real *tzniut* asserts dignity and elegance in the very area that can so easily assert the opposite. When the body shows itself it hides the soul; when it deports itself with a sensitive, delicate and

---

[97] See above, page 29 on King Solomon's writings as transitional.

[98] "Sukkah" (and *s'chach* - the *sukkah's* organic roofing material) is related to this word; the *sukkah* should be transparent - at a deeper level the *sukkah* is a place where a higher reality can be perceived through the medium of the material. The *sukkah's* material substance is flimsy so that it does not obstruct the spiritual (the Zohar calls the *sukkah* "The shade of faith").

dignified elegance it awakens a higher consciousness, it shows that it clothes a soul.

Sarah was a woman whose beauty could lead Egyptians to murder. Yet she was able to carry that same beauty in a way that made Godliness tangible. (Of course to Egyptian eyes no amount of modesty will help - when the eyes are sufficiently fallen, everything is seen in their image.) The vessel can obstruct the light it contains or allow it to shine forth. Sarah was a transparent vessel.

The Beauty of the Human Form
The post-Grecian secular world expresses conflict on the question of sensual beauty: on the one hand the body is exposed, depicted naked in art of all kinds, presented as a classical focus of artistic beauty; on the other, naked exposure of the body is shameful. Those who admire the esthetic of nakedness in art and display such works openly would certainly not themselves appear thus in public; many would go to almost any lengths rather than endure that shame. The sensitivity to nakedness is universal: all cultures cover at least some part of the body.[99] Yet the naked body is depicted as beautiful, and there must be a truth in that. The source of this ambivalence lies precisely in the tension between the two phases of history, the revealed and the hidden. The original beauty of the body is now in captivity.

---

[99] The Greek games were played naked - see page 149, Greece.

V:
New Festivals, New Torah

Chapter 15

Purim

Like Esther's beauty that is transitional, the entire story of Purim describes the transition from revealed to hidden in history, the inversion of modes (*"V'nahafoch hu* - And it was reversed").

At the interface of the periods of the Written and the Oral Law, miracles began to fade. In the days of Mordechai and Esther the miracle of the salvation of the Jewish people was a hidden miracle. The Jews were not saved by an overt interference in the laws of nature. No direct revelation was experienced. Even the prophecy that accompanies that miracle has a muted form – the entire Megilla contains no mention of the Divine Name. To be sure, God is hinted at in the Megilla – we have a tradition that when the Megilla mentions *"hamelech* - the king" (as opposed to "King Achashverosh"), it is a veiled reference to the King of kings, but the point is that the Megilla, unlike the other books of the Written law, does not reveal the Divine name directly.

Purim represents a transition from the revealed to the hidden: on the one hand, it is part of the Written law - there is a Megilla of Esther. But on the other, it has features of the Oral Law. The very name "Esther" means "hidden." The word "Purim" is a Persian word, not Hebrew, and it means "lots" - implying the luck of the draw, suggesting a world detached from Divine providence. In fact there was a debate as to the Megilla's original inclusion in the canon of the Written Law (Megilla 7a); the concern was precisely because it was not clearly prophetic - perhaps it should have been relegated to the type of writings that characterise the Oral Law. The Talmud decides that since prophetic insight is to be found in the Megilla,[100] the question was settled - it belongs in the Written Law. But the point was debatable. Everything about Purim and the Megilla is transitional; it hangs between the prophetic and post-prophetic worlds.

The Megilla of Esther is part of Scripture but its revelation is veiled, and the redemption it documents was not overtly miraculous. The challenge was to see the miracle despite its hidden form. The miracle of the salvation of the Jews at the time of Purim was clothed in seemingly natural events within the political machinations of the Persian court, each of which could have been mere coincidence, that conspired to yield a deliverance; but unlike all former events of salvation, the Divine nature of this one required effort to see. The greatness of the Jews in that generation was that they perceived what was not obvious.

As Dawn Ends the Night

Revealed miracles ended with the era of Purim. No ocean split, no manna fell from Heaven - seemingly natural events conspired to convert destruction to salvation.

Esther is called *ayelet hashachar* - the "gazelle of the dawn" (Psalms 22:1). On this metaphor the *gemara* (Yoma 29a) states: "As dawn ends the night, so Esther ends [the era of] miracles."[101] From her time on, miracles will take the form of apparent coincidence. No longer will natural law be suspended; God will operate in the world only through apparently natural cause and effect.

---

[100] The *gemara* (Megilla 7a) suggests that the Megilla must be prophetic because it contains the verse: "And Haman said in his heart..." - the writer of the Megilla must have had prophetic power to know the private thoughts of a human heart. See there for other proofs and discussion.

[101] The *gemara* then asks: What about Chanuka? That was a later miracle; why is Purim given as the last? The *gemara* answers that Purim was the last miracle *to be written*. Purim ends the phase of Scriptural miracles. Chanuka took place beyond the era of Scripture.

Esther is the end of an era - "As dawn ends the night..." But the metaphor of a breaking dawn seems inappropriate - surely that change should be described as dusk? When miracles end the world goes dark; no longer will flashes of explicit revelation manifest. Why is the end of revelation called a dawn - what new light is being revealed when miracles end and the world goes dark?

Rabbi Yonatan Eybeshutz (Yaarot Devash) deals with this question. A miracle is like a bolt of lightning that illuminates the road at night, briefly, until the next flash. Miracles occur during the night of our journey through the world to make us explicitly aware of the Divine Presence from time to time. During the era of open miracles the world was far brighter than it is now; nature was far more transparent in general. But open miracles were intermittent - from time to time it was necessary to reveal the Divine hand openly. Relative to the spiritual quality of the time, miracles showed much more than the events of the routine passage of time.[102] But once Purim introduced the era of *seeing God's hand within the natural*, intermittent open miracles are no longer needed - now we have the ability to see constantly. To be sure, the intensity of our vision is far less, but a new form of revelation is now permanently available. The point of Purim was to demonstrate Providence within the natural flow of events. Miracles showed the Divine hand openly, Purim showed how to perceive when that hand is withdrawn. Purim introduced a totally new perception into human history. A dawn has broken.[103]

This is precisely our pattern: the era of the Oral Law is far lower than that of the Written. The background illumination is incomparably less. But within that relative darkness we have learned to see in an entirely new way. Previously we lived at a level that made open miracles possible; when we needed to see the Divine hand, it appeared. No effort of perception was needed when that happened; the effort that the times demanded was to maintain a level of purity that made that sort of revelation possible. But after Purim an effort of perception within the darkness reveals the Divine without nature's breaking its rules. We may no longer be able to invoke open miracles, *but we no longer need them.*

---

[102] See Leshem Shvo V'Achlama (Klallim, *klal* 2 *anaf* 3:5) on why miracles are necessary at all.

[103] Maharal titled his work on Purim "Ohr Chadash" ("New Light"); see introductory notes in Y. Hartman edition (Machon Yerushalayim 5774).

The mode of the Oral Law reveals in a radically new way; nature no longer needs to be overridden for the spiritual to be seen - nature can now be seen through. Darkly, imperfectly, with great effort; but it can be done. Dazzling lights no longer flash from the outside, but from within a steady glow can be seen.

"As dawn ends the night, Esther ends the miracles." Open miracles are over; nature will maintain its steady integrity until the Messianic era. The night that was split by flashes of lightning is over. But the dawn of a new, softer, light has broken. A far more subdued light that takes effort and training to see. From now, the Oral Law will reveal a world of subtle miracles.

Torah Received Twice - Sinai and Purim

Every festival reveals new Torah. Purim was not only a salvation, it was also a second giving of the Torah. The two events of giving of the Torah fall into the respective categories of the prophetic and the post-prophetic: the first time the Torah was given, at Sinai, was a completely revelatory experience; no effort was required to perceive that revelation. But the *gemara* states that the real and binding acceptance of Torah was much later, at Purim. The original acceptance of the Torah was forced on the Jewish people by its very clarity; there was no option of ignoring or rejecting it. In fact it could be argued that we should not be not bound by such a coerced event - a contract signed at gunpoint is not valid.[104] That is why the binding acceptance of Torah was at Purim, when there was no coercive revelation, when it would have been easy to interpret events as natural. The significance of the acceptance of the Torah at Purim was precisely in that it was voluntary; no open revelation forced it.

---

[104] At Sinai the mountain was held over the people to force acceptance of Torah (Shabbat 88a). Maharal explains that this was necessary despite the Jewish people's prior voluntary commitment ("We will do and we will listen") in order to demonstrate that the world's existence depends on Torah - it is not optional; the fabric of reality is founded on Torah. Torah is essential and can never be rescinded; it has the force of reality. But the later acceptance of Torah at Purim was truly voluntary - and that is why no claim of coercion can negate its binding status. The first giving of Torah had the clarity of reality itself: a purely first-phase event. The giving of Torah at Purim was entirely voluntary: it was the classical defining event of the second phase of history.

Free Will Under Duress; Repentance Under Pressure

An insight into that voluntary acceptance of Purim is afforded by a question on Rambam's Laws of Sanctifying God's Name. There, Rambam explains that failure to sanctify God's Name in some situations of duress is culpable while in others it is not. The perplexing question, however, is how to distinguish between those categories.

A forced action is not liable. Some situations of force require resistance, even under extreme pressure: there are sins that may not be committed even on pain of death. However, if one succumbs and sins in such situations, the degree of accountability depends: Rambam rules that a sin or crime committed under threat of death is not punishable, even when one is forced to commit idolatry, immorality or murder. Although these three cardinal sins are forbidden even under threat of death, where a person fails to give up his life under threat of death and transgresses, he is not punished (Foundations of Torah 5:4). The transgression was forced on him by the one who threatened to kill him and such force absolves him from statutory punishment (he remains, of course, guilty for the failure to sanctify God's Name - but not for the sin or crime itself, as that was forced upon him).

In the words of Rambam, when under threat of death a person fails to give up his life and commits one of the cardinal sins:

> Despite that, since he transgressed under duress he is not punished... because a person is punished only where he sinned voluntarily...

However, Rambam states that where a *lethal illness* can be cured by resorting to a cardinal sin, one who chooses to save his life by committing that sin is punished appropriately (5:6). Here Rambam states that just as a cardinal sin may not be committed under threat of death, one may not resort to a cardinal sin in order to cure a lethal illness:

> And if he transgressed and was cured by means of the sin, the court punishes him with the appropriate punishment.

What distinguishes these two categories? Why is a sin committed at gunpoint not culpable whereas one committed to avoid death by disease culpable? In both cases the sin is being committed only to save life; why should the form of the threatened death make any difference? Why is a person exempt when he acts to prevent death by a bullet but guilty when he acts to avoid death by an illness?

This well-known question is dealt with by many commentaries on Rambam.[105] The resolution of this apparent contradiction is this: where the force is applied to cause the sin, for example where the victim is forced to sin at gunpoint, he is not culpable because the will expressed in that situation is that of the aggressor. The victim is being forced to act; he is carrying out the aggressor's will, not his own. But where a person is dangerously ill and chooses to sin to save his life, it is *his own will* that is active. The choice to sin is his; no external force is causing him to act – the disease does not force him to sin, it merely threatens to kill; he chooses to sin of his own volition. Of course he does so only to avoid death, but that is his choice. It is true that both scenarios have in common the failure to choose to die; at that level they are parallel. But in one, when the victim chooses not to die he yields to his aggressor's will, whereas in the other when he chooses not to die he acts from his own will. (Indeed, that pivotal point is made precisely in the language of Rambam: "...because a person is punished only where he sinned voluntarily.")

The distinction can be demonstrated as follows: imagine a person woken at gunpoint by an intruder who demands that he unlock his wealthy neighbor's safe to which he has the key. He complies in order to save his life. Would he be held accountable? Certainly not; he yielded his neighbor's valuables only because the alternative was death. But what about this scenario: a person is woken at gunpoint by an intruder who demands that he yield *his own* possessions. The victim says to the intruder: "I have a neighbor who has a safe full of valuables. Let me open his safe so that you can take them..." Would he be liable for his neighbor's loss? Certainly; in this case he offered his neighbor's possessions *of his own will*. To be sure, he was acting under threat, and his action saved his life; but he was not being forced to yield his neighbor's valuables - he *chose* that as the solution to his situation. In the first scenario he acts on the agressor's will; in the second, he acts on his own will.

---

[105] See Minchat Chinuch 296; Ohr Somayach; Chemdat Shlomo, Orach Chaim 38; Seridei Esh II:34 (and 37); R. S. Rozowsky, Zichron Shmuel; Avodat HaMelech.

This distinction illuminates the Jewish people's choice to repent at the time of Purim. At Purim "They established what they had already accepted..." (Shabbat 88a); the definitive acceptance of Torah occurred then, as we have described. At Sinai the mountain was held over them threatening death in the event that they would refuse to accept the Torah. At Purim their repentance and acceptance of Torah was free. But the obvious difficulty here is that *Purim was also a situation of lethal threat:* Haman and the entire Persian empire stood ready to annihilate the Jews. How can repentance in those circumstances be deemed sincere – surely it was done only to escape certain genocide? Why did the threat of death at Sinai negate the binding nature of the acceptance of Torah whereas the threat of death at Purim was not considered forced? Why do we deem the Jewish people forced at Sinai but free at Purim? In both, the alternative options were equally lethal.

The distinction is the one that Rambam has taught. Where a threat directly forces action, that action is not considered an expression of the will of the one who performs it but rather of the agent who applies the force. When God held the mountain over the Jews their acceptance could be deemed legally null: God forced them to accept. But at Purim *no-one forced the Jews to repent or accept Torah;* it is true that they were threatened with death, but no Persian made that death conditional upon non-acceptance of Torah or failure to repent. They were threatened with a complete and unconditional genocide. In that circumstance, when the Jews chose repentance their choice was sincere and valid. No-one forced their return to God and their binding renewal of the Sinai commitment. It is true that the deathly seriousness of their situation awakened their return, and that may well represent a lesser level than totally spontaneous *teshuva* (return); but nevertheless that *teshuva* was of their own volition. They demonstrated a sincere movement towards God; and subsequently the miracle of their salvation awakened a new commitment to Torah in an unprecedented form and with unprecedented intensity. An external threat awakened them, but their return was an expression of their own internal will.[106]

---

[106] This could not be more relevant to us: the *gemara* (Sanhedrin 97b) discusses the parallel *teshuva* that is guaranteed at the end of history: the question is only how much threat will be required to stimulate it.

History's Turning Point
Purim is the inflection point of Jewish history. It ushers in the era of creativity of perception, in Torah as the creative genius of the Oral Law and in the perception of the meaning of history itself as it happens. From now, prophecy from Above will reverberate as an echo in the wisdom of the Sages. A dark world can now be forced to yield some light. What was given before can be created now: the Sages can ordain a new festival - Purim (and later Chanuka) and draw out a new Torah. The reins of Creation have been handed to us.

Purim has a uniquely eternal element. Rambam states (H. Megilla 2:18):

> All prophetic books and sacred writings will be nullified in the Messianic era except the Book of Esther. It will continue to exist like the five books of the Torah that will never cease. Former troubles will fade from memory but Purim will last forever, as it is written: "These days of Purim shall never be repealed among the Jews, and the memory of them shall never cease from their descendants" (Esther 9:28).

Pesach led to the giving of Torah in a blaze of miracles, but the ongoing revelation of that Torah ended with the dying of prophecy. Purim gave us a new Torah, one that illuminates the darkness, a Torah that turns darkness itself into a new light: *"V'nahafoch hu... -* it was reversed."

New Acceptance of Torah: Through Love of the Miracle
The renewed acceptance of the Torah at Purim came about through *"ahavat ha'nes* - love of the miracle" of Purim (Rashi). What is the meaning of "love of the miracle" - and what source is there for such an obligation?

Rambam (Sefer HaMitzvot, Positive Mitzva 3) writes:

> We are commanded to love God. This requires us to think about and contemplate His commandments, sayings and actions until we understand Him and enjoy that understanding with extreme pleasure; that is the love that is obliged.

To think about "His actions" - that will bring about love. Perceiving the revelation of God that the miracle caused was a fulfilment of this injunction. The pleasure of that perception brought about an intense love; witnessing the Purim miracle and understanding its power brought the Jews to a new level of love of God. Purim was an acceptance of the Torah from love.

Sinai was an acceptance in fear: the awesomeness of the Sinai experience obliged that. Force can certainly lead to fear - but not to love. Love can only be evoked as a response, it cannot be obliged. The mode of acceptance of Torah at Sinai was fear; the mode that began the second phase of history at Purim was love. The voluntary acceptance of Torah at Purim evoked by the "love of the miracle" began a new mode of Torah history.

The Fall of Perception
In a dark world, the work of faith takes on new dimensions. When God reveals himself openly, faith is a very different matter than it is when no open revelation is available. The problem of doubt looms large in the post-prophetic age.

Like all second phase phenomena, the history of doubt in human consciousness has its roots deep in the first phase: it began in the Garden. Rambam (Moreh Nevuchim 1:2) records that he was asked this question by a learned individual: How is it possible that Adam sinned and gained as a result? His sin gave him the faculty of "knowing good and evil," a faculty that he did not have previously. Surely his sin should have caused him unqualified demotion; why did he gain the uniquely human and elevated faculty of knowing good and evil as a result of his rebellion?

Rambam answers that the acquisition of the knowledge of good and evil represents a tremendous fall. In truth that knowledge is the result of a precipitous descent. Before the sin, man did not know "good and evil" *because he knew "true and false."* His grasp of reality was so clear that if a thing were lowly or vulgar or in any way bad, he would have related to it as false, non-existent - in fact he would not have seen it. His grasp had the crisp certainty of absolute clarity. After the sin, however, things took on the aspect of good and bad - a far lower version of perception than true and false. Good now does not mean it is the only option; perhaps evil may be worth consideration... And bad is not absolutely proscribed - perhaps it may be worth a thought... Good and bad are perceptions in a world that presents vulgarity and the fallen aspects of the senses as real;

in his former state man would not have been able to perceive such things as having any reality.

Rambam illustrates this notion thus: originally man was naked and knew no shame. All the parts and functions of his body were pure; had you attempted to show him the embarrassing aspect of nakedness he would have been totally unable to understand that. He was blind to that *due to his elevation,* not lowliness. Things were either true or false; there was no concept of good or bad at that level. But after his fall, he perceived the humiliation of the vulgar sensuality that now clung to his body. This new perception of his nakedness had entered his consciousness *because of his lowliness.* His newfound knowledge of good and evil was entirely due to the loss of the piercing clarity of his true-false perception. That was no reward for sin.

Purim and the Problem of Doubt
Doubt entered man's consciousness in the Garden. The *gemara* (Chullin 139b) asks: *"Haman min haTorah minayin* – Where is Haman's name found in the Torah?" It finds Haman's name close to the beginning of the Torah: after Adam eats from the forbidden fruit of the Tree of Knowledge of Good and Evil, God appears in the Garden and asks him: *"Hamin ha'etz...* – Did you eat from the tree...?" The word *"hamin"* is Haman.

When Adam sins, he hides in the Garden. God appears and asks: "Where are you?" and then: "Did you eat...?" The Creator surely knows where Adam is and whether he has eaten. But man is behaving as if God does not see him, and God relates to man only as man relates to Him. Adam has become so confused that he tells himself that he can hide from the One Who sees all. He has entered the dimension of illusion; he has introduced doubt to his world. The consequence is disastrous: now that Adam is imagining that he cannot be seen, God adopts Adam's reality – "Where are you? Did you eat?" as if He does not know. God operates by the rules of the relationship; when man steps away from God, God steps back too. Doubt has entered the world. Man imagines he can hide; God allows him to live in his illusion. From that moment on, nothing will be absolutely clear.

Haman is a descendant of Amalek. Amalek is that mortal enemy dedicated in its essence to destroying the Jewish people. The *gematria* of "Amalek" is *"safek,"* doubt. Amalek attacked the Jewish people as they left Egypt, and Amalek is destined to attack at the end of time in a final attempt to rid the world of Jews. The historic function of the Jewish people is to testify to God's existence in a confusing world: *"Atem eidai – You are My witnesses"* (Isaiah 43:10). Amalek's historic role is to deny that immanence, to keep the gap of doubt open. When man introduces doubt to the world, the root force of Amalek enters the scene; Haman has been born.

Purim was the definitive battlefield on which that historic conflict was fought. As the post-prophetic darkness closed in, the Jews, led by Esther, the woman whose name means hiddenness, chose to see Divine action in the veiled events of their deliverance from Amalek within Persian genocidal persecution. The testimony they bore to that reality laid the foundation for the final victory of certainty over doubt.[107]

The New Work of Faith
The roots of the problem of doubt were planted in the Garden, but doubt came to be the dominant mode of consciousness after Purim. Now we seek proof of a spiritual world and it is not available. To be sure, there is compelling evidence, and any sincere seeker can find it. But the evidence never amounts to absolute proof. That is our intellectual context and that is our challenge. Previously no proof was needed; the spiritual was part of human experience. Now that proof is needed, it is not available. What was obvious truth before must be reconstructed as faith now. The work of faith is to establish a grasp of Torah and commandments based on evidence and immersion in Torah (*emet* - truth), and to assert a powerful loyalty to that truth (*emunah* - faith, or more accurately, faithfulness) in practice.[108]

The primary work required to begin the spiritual path is to see as objectively as possible. Absolute knowledge is not attainable; in fact absolute knowledge is not attainable in any field. The best we can do before committing to action in any area of life is to gather sufficiently compelling evidence; the evidence never amounts to absolute certainty,

---

[107] R. Zadok HaKohen, Machshavot Charutz.

[108] See D. Gottlieb, Reason to Believe (Mosaica Press 2017). See also A. Tatz and D. Gottlieb, Letters to a Buddhist Jew (Targum 2004) p119 and p139. Also "The Thinking Jew's Guide to Life - Faith" (audio presentation by A. Tatz, at simpletoremember.com).

and the best we can do is to predicate action on adequate evidence. Some fields are amenable to better standards of evidence than others, and it is quite possible that evidence for spiritual issues may be harder to establish than for more material ones. But the point remains: commitment is appropriate when the evidence is good enough. The evidence for the claims of Torah are certainly good enough; but one who demands absolute proof will not find it. And one who acknowledges that good evidence is enough in other areas but demands absolute proof in religion is being unrealistic - and possibly insincere.

This is the form that faith must take in the post-prophetic world.

New World, New Conduct
In a darker world where doubt forms the context, a new form of conduct is required. When the spiritual was more revealed, a more spiritual form of conduct was appropriate - even mandatory. The correct response to illness was to seek spiritual help - prayer; or perhaps a visit to a prophet. Visiting a doctor would have been inappropriate; such a *hishtadlut* (effort) would have reflected a serious lack of faith.[109] Now, however, some form of standard medical care is obligatory; relying on the purely spiritual or miraculous is inappropriate. As we move away from the revealed spiritual mode, we are obliged to adopt a more natural mode of *hishtadlut*. Ramban (Vayikra 26:11) states that naturalistic efforts in healing, for example, represent an unacceptable lack of faith; but he is referring to a set of generations or a set of individuals genuinely living at a sufficiently high level.[110] At a much lower level, that conduct becomes irresponsible.[111]

---

[109] King Asa was punished because he consulted doctors (Chronicles II, 16:12). This is Ramban's opinion; Akeidat Yitzchak (26,1) says that Asa's error was his failure to seek Divine help *in addition* to consulting doctors.

[110] There has been much debate about the limits of application of this opinion of Ramban; see J. Kagan, The Choice To Be (Feldheim 2012) p335-344, especially notes 16-19 for a fuller discussion of this and the broader issues.

[111] See Akeidat Yitzchak (26,1) for a lengthy discussion of the appropriate effort required in various life situations.

Another example of new conduct mandated by a new reality is this: there was a time when it was permissible - even laudable - to give away unlimited amounts to charity. People lived on a plane of perception of *hashgacha* (Providence) that enabled them to give away any amount with no fear of their own consequent lack: God provided today, and there is no reason to doubt that He will provide tomorrow. During the Tannaic period however, at Usha, the Sages of the time enacted a law prohibiting the donation of more than a fifth of one's wealth (Ketubot 67b). What was praiseworthy before had now become forbidden. On a sufficiently high plane, certain elevated conduct is appropriate. But at a lower level, that same conduct is problematic; it is no longer in keeping with the prevailing spiritual atmosphere. It will not be genuine; there is no assurance it will be met with a higher *hashgacha* as that level of revealed response has been withdrawn, and such conduct will now be downright irresponsible.

Tanach Jew - Talmud Jew
On a national level, too, new conduct is mandated. In Biblical times the Jewish national mode of conduct was open and dominant - when enemies rose against the Jewish nation, the response was war. King David waged many wars; attacks on the Jewish nation were met with royal and national force. In post-Biblical times however, when the Jewish people's context became exile, the appropriate conduct became very different: anti-Jewish attacks required much more subtle resistance. Chanuka ended the phase in which war was appropriate or even possible; during the long years of exile that response became impossible and a new form of defence became necessary - a strategic working from within the strictures of exile using intellectual and diplomatic creativity. When Jewish national independence ended and the world was given into the control of wicked oppressors, that type of defence became the only one available. History has moved steadily into a mode of *"Eretz nitna b'yad rasha* - The world is given into the hand of the wicked" (Job 9:24), and when the shoe is on that foot, full-frontal attack is no longer the correct response (and of course, through most of Diaspora history, it was physically impossible). It has been said that these two phases of Jewish national conduct are represented by two personae: the "Tanach Jew" and the "Talmud Jew;" the first dealt with resistance in a proud and open fashion as the dignity of Torah and Judaism demanded; the second was obliged to "walk between the raindrops" of constant genocidal storms as a matter of practical wisdom and survival in an exile that presented little alternative.

Chapter 16

From Rebuke to Flattery

One of the features of a world moving away from uncompromising adherence to the truth was the transition from rebuke to flattery. Truth demands rebuke: when someone has behaved badly, truth demands that they be confronted with the inconsistency between their behavior and what is right. Flattery consists in telling a person that they are flawless when that is false.

The *gemara* (Sotah 41a/b) states:

> When King Agrippa [publicly] read [the verse]: "You shall not appoint a foreigner over you" tears flowed from his eyes [because he was not of Jewish origin]. The people said to him: "Do not fear Agrippa, you are our brother, you are our brother..." At that moment the Jews incurred extreme culpability for flattering Agrippa. Said Rabbi Shimon ben Chalafta: "From the day that the fist of flattery arose, law has been distorted, [all] deeds have been corrupted, and no-one can say to his fellow 'My deeds are greater than yours...'" [because the insincerity of flattery distorts everything]. Rabbi Elazar said: "Any person who flatters brings wrath to the world, as it says: 'Those with flattering hearts bring about wrath.' And furthermore, his prayer

> is not heard, as it says: 'They do not pray [even] when they are afflicted.'" And Rabbi Elazar says: "Any person who has flattery within him, even fetuses in their mothers' wombs curse him..."

(The *gemara* goes on to describe other disastrous consequences of flattery.)

Why are flatterers cursed by unborn children? (And why is flattery called a "fist"? A more appropriate metaphor might seem to be a velvet glove...)

There is one other passage in the Talmud (Sanhedrin 91b/92a) where a similar curse is mentioned:

> Rav Yehuda said in the name of Rav: "Anyone who withholds *halacha* [practical Torah knowledge] from a student, is as if he robs him of his ancestral inheritance, as it says: "Torah was commanded to us by Moses, an inheritance of the congregation of Jacob" (Devarim 33:4). It is the inheritance of all Israel from the six days of Creation. Said Rav Chana bar Bizna in the name of Rabbi Shimon Chassida: "Anyone who withholds *halacha* from a student, even fetuses in their mothers' wombs curse him.."

What do these two have in common? A third passage (Nidda 30b) will shed light on this perplexing issue:

> Rabbi Simlai expounded: "What is a fetus like in its mother's womb?...[a description of fetal anatomy and physiology follows; then:] There is a light above his head by which he sees from one end of the world to the other... and there are no days [in human life] more idyllic than these, as it says: "Who could give me like the months of yore, like the days when God protected me?" (Job 29:2), and which time of life consists of months that are not years? These are the months of gestation. And the fetus is taught the whole Torah... Then, during birth, an angel strikes him on his mouth and causes him to forget the whole Torah...

The essence of the human condition is to experience a phase of idyllic perfection during which all wisdom is imprinted into the human psyche and spirit, with no effort, to be followed by a painful loss of that state before moving into a second phase where only extreme effort will recover that original enlightenment. That is the secret of human life. There is always a first phase of a gift from Above, and there is always a cruel withdrawal of that gift. But it is only because the inspiration is withdrawn that the work of genuine achievement can begin; that is the real purpose of life. In fact the gift of wisdom is not removed: it is driven deep into the subconscious. The work of life is to recover one's own original wisdom, to draw it out of one's own intellect and conscience.[112]

It is all locked within. When one learns something deeply true one does not have a feeling of learning, one has a feeling of recognition: *"I know that is true..."* What is happening is that the teaching is resonating with a deep inner knowledge and bringing it to the surface. A good teacher does not put knowledge into the student (that is indoctrination); a good teacher brings it out (that is education).

All life follows this pattern. Relationships have two phases: a romantic phase of inspiration that is the result of no work at all, followed by a phase of real love - but only if much work is done after the romance fades. Childhood is an inspired time; but it does not last - it must be followed by the hard work that maturity demands.[113]

And of course, Jewish history has two phases - the inspired phase of prophecy and miracles, followed by the long centuries of effort to find our way in the darkness and create light itself.

The human fetus represents the essence of this theme: poised at the pivotal transition from the first phase of life's experience to the second. That is precisely the human form that must curse those who obstruct the human project: one who withholds Torah from a student is perverting that student's life essence - that student was created to have Torah taught to him as a fetus and then lose it so that he can struggle to acquire it for his

---

[112] The Vilna Gaon quotes a Midrashic source that states that as you move from this world to the next in the process of death, three angels come to greet you. One comes to add up all your mitzvot, one to add up all your transgressions, and a third to make a global assessment of what you have achieved during life. The Gaon says that as that third angel approaches, you recognize him: he turns out to be the one who taught you Torah in the womb - and now, at the end of life, he is coming to see whether you actualised the potential that he was charged with giving you.

[113] See A. Tatz, Living Inspired (Targum 1993) for an extended discussion of this topic.

own, and this unwilling teacher is preventing that. One who flatters is obstructing the human growth that a flawed individual desperately needs - that individual has fallen away from his own pre-birth perfection; he is failing to live up to his innate potential and what he most needs now is someone to point out that flaw so that he can correct it, and this flatterer is telling him that he is already perfect. The flatterer is doing nothing less than blocking his growth to perfection. The fetus is that form of the human that most intensely feels the shock of being deprived of perfection so that, aware of its deficiency, it can begin the journey back. The fetus, that form of the human who represents the essence of human destiny at the beginning of its journey, curses these obstructers of that destiny.

Flattery is no velvet glove. It is a mailed fist beating back the human project. Rebuke is a key to perfection; but it is a lost art in a post-truth world. Rambam (H.Teshuva 4:2) rules that every community is required to appoint an individual to rebuke them (it takes little imagination to understand why we do not attempt this today):

> Isaiah rebuked Israel and said: "Woe, sinful people..." And God commanded him to rebuke, as it is said: "Cry out in your throat, do not hold back;" and similarly all the prophets rebuked Israel until they repented. Therefore every community should appoint a senior, wise and elderly Sage who has been God-fearing from his youth, who is beloved by them, who will rebuke them and cause them to repent...

Chapter 17

Israel and Greece

Purim introduced the era of doubt. When the Persian exile ended and power passed to the Greeks, doubt hardened to atheism.

In the first phase of history the mode was worship, the question was only what would be worshipped - would it be the true God or false gods, but it was worship nonetheless; in the second phase of history, the mode is atheism. The dominant mode is existential emptiness; I am all that there is, worship is no longer relevant. Now I define my own reality.

Greece stands at the line of transition from idolatry to atheism, from Divine wisdom to human wisdom. Chanuka closely follows the ending of prophecy; Purim was just inside that phase, Chanuka just outside it.

The rise of Greece coincides exactly with the ending of prophecy. These are the words of Rabbi Nissim Gaon in his introduction to the Talmud as he documents the descent of Rav from the land of Israel to Bavel at the beginning of the period of the Amoraim:

> His descent to Bavel was five hundred years after the ending of prophecy *(mi'pisuk ha'nevua)* which occurred [precisely] at the beginning of the rule of Alexander; he went after the establishment of the Second Temple [period], five hundred and thirty years after the [first] Destruction; at that time the Mishna was written [codified in written form by Rabbi Judah the Prince and his contemporary Sages].

Rav Nissim goes on to detail the transmission of the Mishna and the *gemara* until Rav Ashi and Ravina ended the period of the Talmud, some three hundred years after Rav's descent to Bavel:

> Rav Ashi and Ravina were the last of the Amoraim, and Ravina died in the eight hundred and eleventh 'year of documents' *(li'shtarot),* that is, [there were eight hundred and eleven years] from the closing of prophecy *(pisuk ha'nevua)* until the sealing of the Talmud...

The "year of documents" is a reference to the system of dating legal documents that was adopted beginning with the closing of prophecy *(minyan shtarot* - "dating of documents").[114] So major and clear-cut was that event in Jewish consciousness that it required a new dating of history from then; an era had ended and the marking of time itself began anew. The first year of documented history from that time became not the year of Creation, but the year after prophecy ended; the previous era had receded into a dimension too high and too distant to relate to in everyday life.

When Alexander met Shimon HaTzaddik (Yoma 69a) and agreed not to destroy the Temple, he did so on condition that the Jews would begin their dating system from that year (and that Jewish boys born that year would be named Alexander).

So the last year of prophecy and the first year of the reign of Alexander were precisely coincident (that year was exactly one thousand years after Sinai). This is no accident. The ending of prophecy and the beginning of the dominion of Greece are deeply intertwined. The loss of connection with a higher world is precisely what makes it possible for the world to enter a conceptual reality that is entirely bounded by the natural. Greece was able to introduce the materialist view that survives to this day because the palpable evidence for an expanded reality had receded, slipped behind the veil of nature to be hidden until the Messianic era at the end of history will reveal it again.

---

[114] That dating was used until very recently - in the Yemenite community, marriage contracts were dated that way until the current generation.

Our natural mode of thought now is Greek. The modern Western context is pervasively Greek - virtually all modern scientific, political, social, intellectual, philosophical and esthetic structures are based solidly on Greek foundations. The modern mind is built on those foundations. Greece gave the world glorious tools, powerful enough to frame human thought and endeavor for millennia. But the price of those mighty and elegant tools was the closing of the gates to the greater world of the spirit.

Science and Miracles
Modern science is a central part of the legacy of Greece,[115] and it frames all of our thinking. The modern Western view is that science is the only path for seeking and defining truth. The materialist view arrogates to itself the right to define reality - if something claims to be outside science it *must* be false. Materialism is one view, but it claims all of reality. This is the legacy of Greece and the point of the battle between us.

Greece taught the world that only things that can be measured or calculated are real.[116] Modern science excludes miracles; it defines them out of existence. The modern response to the Torah's description of miracles is highly sceptical. Within the current scientific paradigm, miracles could not have occurred. The laws of science govern reality, and therefore miracles are not, *could not,* be real. But that is unreasonable: the claim for a miracle is that it occurs *outside the realm of science* - surely science can say nothing about that! The proper domain of science is the empirical measurement of phenomena and the search for laws that describe their consistency *within the observable universe;* science cannot comment on the claim that there is a fundamental non-observable reality. The claim that a temporary suspension of scientific law occurred is something that science must be silent about; for science to rule that out would be to go beyond its brief - science can have something meaningful to say only about things that fall within its legitimate domain. The

---

[115] See A. Le Roi, The Lagoon (Bloomsbury 2014) for an extended account of how Aristotle laid the foundations of modern science.

[116] Ramban (Vayikra 16:8): "...those who follow the Greek [Aristotle] who denied all that was beyond his grasp, and prided himself (he and his students...) in thinking that anything that they could not attain with their intellect is not true..."

modern view takes for granted that miracles contradict science, but that is just plain wrong - miracles do not contradict science, *they stand outside of science*.[117] When science *a priori* rules out phenomena beyond its borders it is effectively stating that *nothing is beyond its borders*. That is unreasonable *in scientific terms* - the claim that science rules out the miraculous is a misunderstanding of what science is.

Scientific laws are not legal laws: a law in the legal sense is prescriptive - things must be a certain way because the law requires it. But a law of science is descriptive - it simply states a maximally economical and fitting pattern to a set of observations. A law of science holds together a set of phenomena in a descriptive frame; it may indeed predict future events of the type it has described, but it does not mandate that those events fit the law - it can only *expect* them to do so. If the next observation contradicts the law, the law will simply have to be modified; it will then be apparent that it was formerly incomplete and a new or broader law will have to be formulated. The point is that the laws of science do not fix reality, they merely describe it after the fact.[118] When a miracle supervenes, scientific law is temporarily set aside; that is what a miracle does. There is nothing inherent in scientific law that prohibits miracles. Miracles occur in a zone beyond science's tools of measurement and explanation.

The scientific method begins with the observation of facts; science observes what it can observe and comes to conclusions that best fit those observations. When its conclusions go beyond the realm of the observed facts, science has overstepped its mark. When science presumes to exclude the supernatural it has openly declared that it alone has the right to define the totality of reality. That way of seeing the world is almost the only way possible for modern minds formed in the image of Greece, minds that have lost their connection with the larger world of the spirit. But it is a view of the world that is born of a time and a culture, not of

---

[117] "Creationism" or "Creation science" sometimes presents scientific evidence for Biblical miracles (for example, evidence of a widespread flood that could correlate with the Biblical Flood). This is a mistaken enterprise: the Flood was a miraculous event (Midrash Rabba) - it stood outside of science; there is no reason to expect natural evidence. To demand natural evidence for supernatural events is to confuse categories.

[118] See below, page 153: What Are Laws of Nature?

logical necessity. At root it is a choice to see the world in a particular way.[119]

What Are Laws of Nature?
In fact, there is a debate among philosophers about whether laws of nature simply describe reality ("regularity" theory) or indeed underlie reality in a causal sense ("necessitarian" theory). On the regularity theory, laws simply describe the way the world is. In fact, on this theory, strictly speaking, regularity itself is not required - whatever happens in the world is captured by the law. (It has been pointed out that on this theory, free will presents no problem: whatever is chosen is what happens, and the law simply describes what happens.) By this account there is no reason that anything *has to be* a certain way in the first place. By the same token, miracles present no problem - if they happen in the world, then that is simply the way the world is and no law can prevent that (because on this view, laws have no controlling hold on reality; they simply describe it).

According to the necessitarian view, laws express underlying patterns that condition reality. The world *must be* the way the laws determine. It is true that the laws can only be inferred from observation of the way the world is, but once the law has been correctly expressed, reality must follow the law. To be sure, this view has nothing to say about *why* the laws are what they are in the first place, but nevertheless they have authority. But even on this view, miracles cannot be ruled out: miracles obey their own set of laws, and those laws interact with the natural ones in a manner determined entirely lawfully.[120] The laws of miracles allow natural law to operate, but cause miracles to break into the natural order when necessary.

Either way, miracles stand outside of nature. They operate according to their own set of laws which interact with the natural order under Divine control no less meticulous than that which governs the natural.

From a Torah perspective, the debate is moot: there certainly are laws that govern the universe. There is a deeply causal root underlying all of

---

[119] See the quote on page 20.

[120] Maharal, Second Introduction to Gevurot Hashem.

reality (natural and supernatural) - and that root is Torah. The world is the way it is because Torah is the way it is; and Torah is the way it is because God wills it that way.

A Conditional Creation
The mechanism of revealed miracles was built into creation from the beginning. God created all phenomena of the natural world with that condition: they will follow natural law until a miracle is required - and then they will adopt the mode of the miraculous. The miraculous is just as much part of the structure of reality as the natural.[121]

When the sea split to allow the Jewish people to travel and to drown the Egyptians, the verse states: *"V'chazar ha'yam l'eitano* - And the sea returned to its strength," meaning that when the need for miraculous splitting was over, the sea returned to its natural state. The Sages hear another meaning in the word *"l'eitano"* - besides the more obvious one of "to its strength," the letters of the word can be rearranged to mean "to its condition," meaning to the condition that was built into the nature of the sea at its original creation. During the six days of Creation, when God created the ocean, He made its nature conditional: to operate horizontally according to the natural laws of physics for most of its history, *on condition* that when needed, it would defy those laws and stand vertically. Thus during the Exodus when the time came for the Jews to be saved from the Egyptians the sea fulfilled that miraculous condition, and when that need was over the sea returned to its original natural state.

(On one of Rabbi Chaim of Volozhin's visits to his teacher the Vilna Gaon, he took along his son Itzele, who was six or seven years old at the time. One of the questions that Rabbi Chaim asked the Gaon on that occasion was this: "If the ocean was created with an inbuilt condition for the miraculous, that condition must be located in Torah - we should be able to identify a verse indicating the creation of that condition. After all, everything is in Torah: if God created such a condition as part of the creation of the ocean, the Torah must say so. Where do we find such a verse?" Before the Gaon could answer, young Itzele tugged at his father's

---

[121] See Leshem Shvo v'Achlama (Klallim, *klal* 2, *anaf* 3) for an extended and seminal discussion on the condition underlying nature and the purpose of miracles in general, including the later miracles of the Oral Law period (includes references to all the major commentaries on these issues).

sleeve: "Father, why ask the *tzaddik* - why not ask me?" The Gaon turned to the boy and said: "Speak," and the child proceeded to give this answer: "Describing the original creation of the oceans in Genesis, the verse says: *'Yikavu hamayim mi'tachat ha'shamayim el makom echad, v'tera'e ha'yabasha* - Let the waters under the heavens be gathered unto one place, and let the dry land be revealed.' Well, if the waters are gathered unto one place, obviously dry land will be revealed. The Torah would not go on to state the obvious. Therefore, when the Torah goes on to say 'and let the dry land be revealed,' it must be referring to *another occasion* on which dry land will be revealed where the ocean once was..." The Gaon kissed the boy as a sign of agreement.)

Such a condition was inserted into all parts of Creation, not only the ocean (B. Rabba 5:5):[122]

> Rabbi Yochanan said: God made a condition with the ocean that it would split before Israel. Rabbi Yirmiya ben Elazar said: Not only with the ocean did God make a condition, but with all that was created in the six days of Creation...

All things are governed by two sets of laws: the natural for most of their history, and the miraculous for those rare moments when they will be required to reveal a higher reality.

The reason for this condition is *"Ein kol chadash tachat ha'shemesh* - There is nothing new under the sun." All was known and planned; the Divine system does not require emergency adjustments to correct for unforeseen deviations. All necessary aspects of Creation were in place from the beginning.

---

[122] It is no accident that Torah reveals the condition inherent in all things here, at the splitting of the ocean. The condition underlying the nature of the oceans is deeply fundamental: the primeval waters split to make a place on earth for man in the original Creation, that action was repeated after the Flood for the creation of a second edition of mankind, and it was repeated again for the formation of the Jewish people at the Exodus. In fact every human is born as a result of the breaking of the waters of the womb during labor; and Moses was drawn from the waters of the Nile (see Maharal, Gevurot Hashem, Exodus 18 and Leshem Shvo v'Achlama, Sefer ha'De'ah Part 2, *drush* 5, *anaf* 2:7-9 on the deeper meaning of this pattern).

But this raises a basic question: why are *miracles* required to move history towards its final goal - could that project not be ensured by natural means? Why was it necessary to split an ocean to save the Jewish people - it is not hard to imagine any number of Divine interventions clothed in natural form that would have achieved that end. Why build all of reality with miracles in the first place; it is surely not beyond God's ability to run the program of history without recourse to the miraculous.

Leshem answers that all of the Creation has only one goal: to manifest *kavod Shamayim* - the glory of Heaven. That is the driving force behind all that takes place in the world, hidden throughout most of history, but moving all things inexorably towards that goal nevertheless. All of history moves towards a final revelation of that glory, and that end is guaranteed regardless of how human free will may bend the path that leads to it. When history threatens to subvert that goal *it will be brought back to that path* - a miracle will manifest, showing that such failure is ruled out absolutely. When the Egyptians pursue the Jewish people threatening to thwart their historic journey to Sinai and beyond, the world faces the possibility of the failure of its intended destiny. That cannot be; at that time an abrogation of nature itself will manifest to show that all the objects and laws of Creation were put in place only for that journey to come to its completion. History will be put back on track; not subtly and invisibly, but openly and publicly demonstrating that the laws that govern nature are forever bonded to moving the world towards its ultimate goal.

All things exist on condition that they will serve that purpose. "There is nothing new under the sun" because at the beginning the goal was set - and that will never change; nothing moves outside the boundaries of that project, and if it becomes necessary to break natural law to keep that process on track, natural law will be broken.

The Creation exists only on the condition that Torah is accepted:

> *Hitna haKadosh Baruch Hu im maasei Bereishit...* - The Holy One made a condition with the Creation and said to it: "If Israel accepts the Torah you will continue to exist, and if not I shall return you to the void" (Shabbat 88a).

That condition is ongoing - Torah must be learned and observed constantly to sustain existence: "If not for My covenant day and night, I would not have set the laws of heaven and earth in place" (Jeremiah

33:25) - Nefesh HaChaim (5:11) states that if the world would ever experience even a moment during which Torah is not active, it would cease to exist.

Torah is a revelation of God's glory; that is the purpose of Creation ("*Ha'kol bara li'ch'vodo* - He created everything for His glory"), and all things exist to fulfil it. Whatever form the world needs to make that happen will be the form that it takes - natural or miraculous. Since all was created for that goal, the existence of every thing rests on the condition that it will move towards that goal. If that can be achieved through natural law, that will be the law that operates; if that can be achieved only through the miraculous, then the miraculous will operate.

A Higher Order
The higher order that governs the miraculous is the Jewish people's historical context; we live in the domain of the miraculous (Rabbi Yaakov Emden writes that in his opinion, the survival of the Jewish people and the preservation of its Torah against all odds is a greater miracle than those of the Exodus). We celebrate our birth as a nation by recounting our miraculous origin - Rambam (H. Chametz u'Matza 7:1) rules that the obligation of the Passover *seder* is this:

> It is a positive mitzva of the Torah to tell about the miracles and wonders that happened to our Fathers in Egypt on the night of the fifteenth of Nissan...

Here, Rambam does not specify an obligation to mention the Exodus itself - only the miracles that accompanied it, even though the verse that he quotes as the source for this law states clearly: "Remember this day, on which you left Egypt (Exodus 13:3)." Evidently, Rambam understands that the mitzva of telling of the Exodus is performed by telling of its miracles. The reason for this is that the essence of the story of the Jewish people's formation is not a geographical story of movement from one place to another (Egypt to Israel) nor a political story of movement from one political condition to another (slavery to freedom), but a story of movement from one reality to another - from the natural to the miraculous. Maharal points out that we spend Passover night telling of miracles - that is, the shattering of order, and we call that ceremony a *"seder"* - meaning "order." The Jewish people are at home on the supernatural plane; *that* is our order.

Conditions for Rabbinic Miracles?
We do not find a discussion of inbuilt conditions when it comes to the miracles performed by the Sages. The Sages were able to bend the natural world to their will without requiring any pre-existing conditions. The reason for this is that all of Creation is for the purpose of revealing Divine glory *by means of humans*. Man is here to use the Creation for that purpose; when he needs some part of the world to behave in a particular way to achieve that end, he has the right to force it to behave that way regardless of natural law. The natural world was created in the first place only to be used by man for its ultimate purpose; that is the deepest of all its laws.

The *gemara* (Chullin 7a) demonstrates this principle:

> Rabbi Pinchas ben Yair was travelling [on a mission] to redeem captives. He came to the River Ginai. He said to the river: "Ginai, split your waters so that I may cross over." The river said to him: "You are doing the will of your Creator and I am doing the will of my Creator. Perhaps you will succeed, perhaps you will not succeed [your success in doing your Creator's will is doubtful]. I, however, am certainly doing [my Creator's will]." [The river thus refused to split.]
>
> Rabbi Pinchas said to the river: "If you do not split I shall decree that no water will ever flow in you again."
>
> The river split for him.
>
> Another man was present who was carrying wheat for Passover. Rabbi Pinchas said [to the river]: "Split for him too because he is performing a mitzva." The river split [again]. There was an Arab merchant accompanying them. Rabbi Pinchas said [to the river]: "Split for him too so that he should not accuse us of abandoning fellow travellers." The river split [again].
>
> Rav Yosef said: "That man [Rabbi Pinchas ben Yair] was greater than Moses and the six hundred thousand [Jews who left Egypt] because there [at the splitting of the sea] it happened only once [the sea split for the Jews once] whereas here it happened three times..."

This exchange between the Rabbi and the river raises questions. Firstly, the river's argument is flawed: it asserts that since Rabbi Pinchas' success is doubtful, he may not be doing his Creator's will - but that is wrong: he is certainly fulfilling his Creator's will by attempting to redeem captives. Whether or not he succeeds is not the issue; that is up to God, not him. His mitzva is to try; he is certainly doing that. Why does the river not see that? Secondly, why does he choose to ignore the river's challenge and simply threaten it? The river has raised an apparently cogent argument; why not answer it? If the argument is flawed, why not point that out? Why resort to force?

The answer to these questions depends on understanding the purpose of the natural world. The river expresses its nature - it was created to flow and it is doing that. It has no mitzva obligations; redeeming captives is not its problem, and therefore it sees no need to change its nature. It does not see things from the point of view of fulfilling mitzvot. Rabbi Pinchas ben Yair is a human with obligations; he is in the process of fulfilling one of them. The material world is there for him to use as he sees fit to accomplish his purpose - he has the authority to dictate to the world how it should behave to serve him. Faced with that authority, the river obeys his command - its everyday nature is indeed simply to flow, but its deeper nature is to serve the *tzaddik* to fulfil the purpose of Creation. The correct answer to the river's challenge is precisely to use it for that purpose.

No specific condition is needed to make that behavior possible; it is enough that the entire material world was created for this - that is its essential nature.

When God operates in the world during the era of prophecy, the prophet is the agent through which God speaks (in prophecy) or acts (in miracles). God speaks and acts through prophets because the world was built solely so that its perfection will be revealed by humans. There is no point in Creation's moving to its destiny without human agency; the reason for Creation was to give man that task - and its reward. That is why miracles require human agency; both in the prophetic and post-prophetic eras. When miracles occur during the prophetic era the prophet is the medium of that revelation. The miracle is a manifestation of God in the world - and He does not create anything new under the sun: if a miracle occurs, its potential must have been built into the original Creation.

However, in the phase of the Oral Law the Sages are in control; they move Creation forward on their own initiative, they can demand that the objects of Creation obey for that purpose, and no particular condition is needed - all objects were created in the first place to serve man in his task of perfecting the world in order to reveal its Divine Source.

"There is nothing new under the sun" when God operates in the world; all the conditions needed for later change were set in place from the beginning. But when man operates independently in the phase of the Oral Law, *he can bring new things about* without any prior condition. The only condition he needs is the deep nature of Creation itself: all things are for the purpose of revealing God in the world by man's actions, and provided man is doing that work he can use the world as he sees fit - naturally or miraculously.[123] *"Tzaddik gozer v'haKadosh Baruch Hu mekayem* - The righteous person decrees and God fulfils" (see Tanchuma Vayera 19; Zohar Genesis 45; Moed Katan 16b; Taanit 23b). This is another aspect of the Sages' superiority over the Prophets *(chacham adif mi'navi)*.

Sanctity of Joshua, Sanctity of Ezra

Leshem (Klallim, *klal* 2, *anaf* 3:9) states that this superiority is the reason that the sanctity that Ezra brought about on his entry to the Land of Israel was superior to that of Joshua's. Joshua's sanctity *(kedusha rishona* - the "first sanctity") did not last; it dissipated with the exile that followed the first Temple's destruction. Ezra's sanctity *(kedusha shni'a* - "second sanctity") however, did not end with the second Temple's destruction and consequent exile; it remains to this day. The surprising strength of the second *kedusha* relative to the first, states Leshem, is due to the special powers given to the Sages of the Second Temple era:

> We can understand the Sages' reasoning when they say: *"Kedusha rishona* (the 'first sanctity') was sanctified for its own

---

[123] Compare Maharsha *ad loc* who suggests a source for the condition inherent in Creation that allows the river to split for Rabbi Pinchas ben Yair. While it is true that all is contained in Torah and no doubt a source can be found, it is not necessary - when the Sages assume control of the natural world by virtue of their Torah, they can dictate its behavior. The consideration of "nothing new under the sun" that mandates preconditions for God's miracles does not constrain the Sages of the Oral Law; they are able to bring new things into being as they deem appropriate (Leshem Shvo vAchlama, Klallim, *klal* 2, *anaf* 3:10).

time but was not sanctified for the future, whereas *kedusha shn'ia* (the 'second sanctity') was sanctified for its own time and also for the future (and Rambam rules thus as *halacha*...). At first sight this is amazing - the *kedusha rishona* was initiated by the entire Jewish people, the revealed *Shechina*, the *aron* and its cover, the *keruvim* and the *Urim v'Tumim*... and they entered [the Land] with Joshua and the Elders and with miracles and wonders, whereas the *kedusha shn'ia* lacked all of these. How is it possible that that the *kedusha shn'ia* should have a greater effect than the *kedusha rishona*? But according to what we have explained this is understood; for at the [time of the] second entry [into the Land] God gave them control over the entire Creation... All the gates of Torah... were open before them. And God agreed to all that they did, as stated in Megilla 7a: *"kiymu v'kiblu* - they upheld and accepted" meaning that it was upheld Above what they accepted below. Therefore the sanctity that they generated at the second [entry into the Land] was sanctified for its own time and for the future.[124]

The Materialist Choice
Greece introduced a worldview that rules out the miraculous. Not only the miraculous: even an immaterial soul is a dubious proposition in that view. Torah sees the material world as only the outer face of a far deeper reality.

A culture that chooses materialism as its defining mode and decides *ab initio* that there is nothing behind the empirically observed facts of the world has chosen to see only the outer garments of reality. But worse than that: it has confused the garments for essence. To start by ruling out all possibility of meaning and purpose and then study the world assiduously is to miss the point in the most extreme way. A culture that focuses on science after deciding that nothing lies behind the science and that the body is all there is (and that the mind cannot be more than a function of the body) is like an observer with sealed ears at a musical

---

[124] The Vilna Gaon points out that the name "Joshua" means "God saves" - Joshua lives in the prophetic era and all that manifests in the world is done by God. The name "Ezra" means "God helps" - in Ezra's era man is empowered to act independently; God only helps.

ISRAEL AND GREECE / 161

concert paying close attention to the appearance of the musicians, their instruments and dress, the decor and lighting, the movement of hands and baton - but deaf to the music.[125] That observer has seen accurately, his observations are faultless and his report will be a model of objectivity, but he has missed the point spectacularly.[126]

And yet that view of the world has great beauty. Greece presented an extremely attractive culture, it offered new tools for the intellect, powerful esthetics and a majestic philosophy. So powerful was the Hellenistic attraction that Jews were swept away by it. Even major figures could be vulnerable - Rabbi Elisha ben Avuya ("Acher"), no less than a colleague of Rabbi Akiva's who had entered the mystical *Pardes* ("Orchard") with him was lured away by it.[127] It must have been awesomely powerful to attract a person of that stature.

Greece aimed to extinguish the light of the transcendent and start again with human experience and intellect as its only tools. That is the defining characteristic of the second phase; Greece was the nemesis of the Great Assembly and its Torah - Greece taught the world to define reality solely by the measure of human understanding and empirical experiment. Prior to that age wisdom was drawn down from the higher worlds; Greece cut the world off from that source. Prior to that era man's inner reality was defined by God; now it is defined by man. In the world that Greece gave us, prophecy will not speak to enlighten us; miracles will not occur to convince us. We are on our own.

---

[125] See J. Kagan, The Choice To Be (Feldheim 2012) pp347-350 who formulates this analogy in a different context.

[126] Rabbi Shapira once commented that studying the human condition after deciding *a priori* that man does not have a spiritual component is like cutting off and discarding the head of a dog and then studying what remains and claiming to understand what a dog is. That is not only bad religion; it is bad science.

[127] The *gemara* (Chagiga 15b) states: "Acher - what was his failing? Greek songs *(zemer Yevani)* did not cease from his mouth. They said about Acher that when he stood up [from his learning] in the Bet Hamidrash many heretical books would fall *(noshrin)* from his lap." Rabbi Shapira pointed out that the word *"noshrin"* does not mean to fall in the simple sense but rather in the sense of fruits or leaves detaching from a tree, or feathers from a bird - the nuance is that the heretical books he carried around were part of him.

Chapter 18

Chanuka

Chanuka was the showdown with Greece, the clash of cultures that would shape Western values until the end of history. The events of Chanukah took place when there were no longer prophets and therefore there is no book in Scripture that relates its events. In fact Chanukah is so much part of the process of the Oral Law that it is not even mentioned in the Mishna; it is simply the subject of a discussion in the *gemara*.[128]

Chanuka celebrates the breaking through of the miraculous into a non-miraculous world. Greece taught the world to see with material eyes only; it was concerned with stamping out the spiritual vision of Israel. Greece made no attempt to annihilate the Jews; its quarrel was not with Jews but with Judaism. The war with the Greeks was a war of ideology - Greece was concerned with foisting its worldview on reality for all time, and the heroes of the Chanuka revolt were ready to give their lives for a very different view of reality.

---

[128] The section in the Talmud discussing the Chanukah lights is inserted in a discussion of Shabbat lights (Shabbat 21a). Shabbat represents a process that is entirely given from above, it is *k'viya v'kayma* - fixed and permanent (Pesachim 117b); in no way subject to human adjustment. Chanukah is entirely a process generated from below. Both light the world - together.

Chanuka celebrates the victory of their transcendent worldview. The battle between Greece and Israel was a cosmic battle between the natural and the supernatural. The last revealed miracle of history, the miracle of the oil, was a demonstration that the supernatural lives on.

Chanuka has no *megilla,* and although the miracle of Chanuka was an open miracle it has features of the phase of the Oral Law. The miracle of the war, like the miracle of Purim, did not manifest open abrogations of nature, and in fact required strenuous human effort - a bitter war fought against the Greek Empire that eventually dragged on for years, during which four of the five heroic sons of Mattityahu died. The victory was certainly miraculous: a small band of priests wrested victory from a mighty armed empire, but the war featured no overt change in nature and great human effort was required - these are features of the post-prophetic era.

The overtly supernatural miracle of the oil was private, in the inner precincts of the Temple, utterly unlike the public spectacle of Biblical miracles. It was not a miracle of salvation; it occurred *after* the main stage of the military victory, and it occurred with no prophet present - unlike Biblical miracles. This, the last[129] miracle that we witnessed, was transitional - overtly miraculous like the miracles of the Biblical phase, but its defining features were those of the post-Biblical type of miracle. Chanuka carries the flame of the memory of open revelation into the long darkness of hidden Providence.

It is not accidental that the protagonists of the Chanuka battle were *kohanim* (priests). *Kohanim* stand between two worlds; Maharal points out that the name *"kohen"* signifies the interface between physical and spiritual: *kohen* is equal to seventy-five in *gematria;* a hint at the midpoint between seven and eight, that is between the numbers that represent the natural and the transcendent. *Kohanim* stand between God and the people, representing each to the other - the *gemara* (Yoma 19a) questions whether the *kohanim* are *shluchei d'Rachmana* (agents of God) or *shluchei di'dan* (agents of ours) - the question is whether they

---

[129] There was one revealed miracle after Chanuka: the dead of Betar, who lay exposed due to a Roman edict prohibiting their burial, miraculously did not decompose and were eventually brought to burial. That last of all miracles was a premonition of the redemption, a hint from Above that the dead will ultimately be revived.

represent God to us, or us to God. In fact they serve both functions (the debate is only which is primary). That is precisely the role of the *kohanim:* they are agents of connection to the spiritual. They serve in the Temple, the place of this world's connection to a higher world. They bridge the gap, and it was *kohanim* who led the Chanuka revolt - Greece asserts that the gap is unbridgeable; God may have created the world, but He is now no longer in contact with it. The High Priests of the Chashmonaim demonstrated exactly that ongoing connection. Chanuka was the bridging event of history; it joins the previous miraculous era with the era of nature's reluctance to reveal.

Healing of the Legs
Purim and Chanuka straddle the divide. They are the bookends of the phase of transition - each has features of the revealed and the hidden: the Purim miracle occurred within the phase of the revealed but its nature was that of hidden miracles. Prophets were present and Purim saved the Jewish people, these are features of the miracles of the prophetic era, but no supernatural event occurred. The miracle of the Chanuka oil occurred in the phase of the hidden but its nature was that of the revealed. No prophet was present, and it played no part in saving the Jewish people, but it was a supernatural event. Purim saw the last ebb of the first phase, Chanuka introduced the second.

Purim ends the phase of the Written Law, Chanuka begins the phase of the Oral Law. Together they draw the Written into the Oral. They are the legs of Jewish history (Purim the right leg, Chanuka the left).[130] Here the body ends: Purim and Chanuka do not have the sanctity of Biblical festivals with their prohibition of work; they are external, like the legs that are external to the body proper. But like the legs, they are the agents that carry the body forward. Torah stands on them and walks on them - we move into the future in an ongoing creative process of Torah in the Oral Law that extends the Written.

Mattityahu the High Priest who began the revolt against the Greeks that became the miracle of Chanuka achieved a partial correction of a problem that had begun long before. Arizal states that when Jacob fought with Esau's angel and suffered an injury to his thigh, a weakness set into the Jewish people that would run through history. That injury would remain

---

[130] Arizal, Shaar HaKavanot; Meor Eynaim, Haazinu.

with us as a vulnerability to Esau for centuries. Chanuka effected something of a correction, a healing in the cosmic body of the Jewish people.

(The verse states: *"Vayiga b'kaf yerecho vateka kaf yerech Yaakov* - And he smote his thigh and the thigh of Yaakov was injured." Rabbi Yosef Chaim Zonnenfeld noted that *"vayiga* - he smote" is equal to "Chanuka" in *gematria,* and *"kaf yerecho* - his thigh" is equal to "Purim.")

Esau injures Jacob's thigh; that gives Esau a particular power over us. Esau is the progenitor of Rome, the Empire that will dominate until the Messianic era. Rome propagated Greek culture; it was not a culture unto itself so much as a power based solidly on Greek roots that spread those roots in the world. We are in the grip of Rome, but the driving culture behind Rome is Greece. Esau dominates us with his power and the ideology of Greece. When the Chashmonaim defeated the Greeks, the healing of Jacob's thigh began. Torah was mortally threatened - Jews were defecting *en masse* to Greek culture, enthralled by the beauty and power of the Hellenistic ideal. Torah's journey into the future faced a dire threat. The Chashmonaim met that threat and overcame it - and healed the legs of Jewish history. We continue the journey; still lame, perhaps, but still walking.

The battle with Greece was the battle to assert the culture that would define mankind. Greece aimed to permanently sever any connection with a higher reality, to define the world forever as a system devoid of all relationship with the Absolute. A world formed in the Greek image would have been merely human; world culture would have included no opening to transcendence, no possibility of reaching beyond the boundaries of human philosophy or the finite dimensions of the material. Great and glorious to be sure; intellectually mighty, esthetically inspired, encompassing all of science and technology and always expanding the boundaries of human knowledge - but always limited to the dimensions of the world, never reaching beyond it. And Greece could have done it: in the post-prophetic world the open evidence was all on their side, the tools they had for the job were exquisitely beautiful, and Jews were adopting them enthusiastically.

The Chashmonaim held back a colossal tide; with their self-sacrifice in a world that offered nothing to aid them they did battle with a mighty army and a mighty culture. Unexpectedly they were met by a miracle, a supernatural light that shone briefly in the natural world. But that was enough. Jews are here to declare that the material world is not the sum total of reality, and those heroes demonstrated that even in the post-prophetic darkness an avenue of access to a higher light can be found.

They revealed that the world is not disconnected. Faith lives on; the darkness may be almost overwhelming but as long as a small flame shines in a Jewish window at Chanuka the world remembers that the natural is not everything. A secular culture dominates, and it will dominate until the Messianic destiny is revealed. But in that secular and materialistic reality another message can be heard, and it will continue until the end of history when it will be vindicated.

Chapter 19

A Prophet may not Add

The Talmud (Megilla 14a) states:

> Forty-eight prophets and seven prophetesses prophesied for Israel and they never subtracted from nor added anything to what is written in Torah except for the reading of the Megilla (of Purim).

The problem that the *gemara* addresses here is how Purim could have been added to Torah by the Men of the Great Assembly in the time of Mordechai and Esther: it is strictly forbidden to add to Torah. The prohibition of *"bal tosif* - do not add (to Torah)" should have made that addition impossible. Both the addition of the Megilla of Esther to Scripture and the addition of the new festival of Purim (with its commandments) to Jewish life should be unthinkable in the face of this prohibition. The *gemara* answers that indeed it is forbidden to add, but in this case the Sages found a source for Purim in the Torah itself.[131] This is not really adding; it is merely expanding a compressed source within Torah.

---

[131] See Megilla 14a (and Megilla 7a) for the Torah derivation that allowed adding the Megilla of Purim.

A question that the *gemara* never asks is: "What about Chanuka?" Apparently, the addition of the mitzva of Chanuka raises no difficulty. But this is hard to understand - Chanuka is clearly a mitzva added by the Rabbis of its time. Why does that addition not raise the same question of the prohibition of adding to the Torah?

Rashi raises the question.[132] He comments:

> "Except for the reading of the Megilla." And if you ask: what about the (mitzva of the) Chanuka lights? By then the prophets had ceased to exist; but in the days of Mordechai there were Chaggai, Zecharia and Malachi.

Rashi is saying that the problem of adding is relevant only when prophets exist. Adding the Megilla and the mitzvot of Purim presents a problem only because Chaggai, Zecharia and Malachi (the last three prophets) were alive at the time. That problem requires a solution, and that is why the *gemara* addresses it. But adding to the Torah is no problem at all when prophets no longer live. The addition of the festival and the mitzva of Chanuka contravened no prohibition because "the prophets had ceased to exist." The question of prohibited additions to Torah depends, according to Rashi, on whether or not "prophets exist" at the time that the addition is being made. What does Rashi mean? This certainly requires explanation.

The text of the Midrash (Torat Kohanim, Bechukotai 13) is: *"Elu hamitzvot... she'ein ha'navi rashai lechedash davar ma'ata* - These are the mitzvot... a prophet may not add anything from now..." The point is that a *prophet* may not add. Rashi is clearly going further: it is the *existence of prophets* at the time when an addition is made that is the problem. Why should the prohibition depend not so much on whether it is a prophet who is making the addition, but on the existence of prophets at the time that the addition is made?

The key to grasp here is that during the era of prophecy, adding to the Torah was conceivable - and forbidden. It was conceivable because

---

[132] There are a number of approaches to this question: according to Ramban (Ramban, Beha'alotecha; see also Nefesh HaChaim 1:22) in depth Chanuka is also derived from Torah: Chanuka was revealed to Aharon. Neither Purim nor Chanuka are illicit additions because both are ultimately derived from Torah.

prophecy is precisely the mode that reveals Torah; all Torah is prophecy. If there is anyone who could add to Torah, it could only be a prophet. But when prophets no longer exist *nothing could possibly be added to Torah.* In the phase of the Oral Law all that the Sages can do is draw a new understanding of Torah from the depths of their own hearts and minds. Purim was not "added" - it was latent within Torah and revealed by the Sages. Chanuka is added, but it is not an addition to Torah. The Written Torah is complete and sealed; now that prophecy has ceased there is no possibility of adding to the body of prophecy that is Torah. Rashi is saying that Purim is added to Torah from within Torah; Chanuka is added after Torah ends.

The mitzva of Chanuka is created by the Sages as a product of their judgment; it is not part of Torah in the same sense as those parts written and created when prophets and prophecy were alive and revealing Torah. Just as the Sages could initiate miracles of their own accord in the phase of the Oral Law,[133] they could initiate the observance of Chanuka - just as miracles that previously revealed God in the world now reveal the independent creative power of the Sages; similarly this new mitzva is not being inserted into Torah but being expressed at a far lower level, the level of distant independence that characterises the Oral Law. Chanuka is added *after* Torah has been sealed - "Chanuka is the festival of the Oral Law" (R. Hutner, Pachad Yitzchak, Chanuka *ma'amar* 4).

The addition of Chanuka does not transgress the prohibition of *bal tosif* (adding to Torah) any more than any later edict or public enactment of the Sages. Inserting Purim into Torah (both as a text in Scripture and as a new festival in Jewish life, with its mitzvot) needs explanation; unless it can be discovered already within Torah it would certainly be a prohibited addition. Adding Chanuka to Judaism needs no explanation; when prophecy has died nothing can be added and the problem does not arise.

Every redemption reveals new Torah. Just as the Exodus from Egypt led to an acceptance and hence a revelation of Torah in the world, so the redemption of Purim led to a new acceptance and a new revelation of Torah. (Maharal, in Tiferet Yisrael 32, states that acceptance of a new mitzva constitutes a new acceptance of the whole Torah - that is Purim: a new acceptance of the whole Torah.) Both Purim and Chanuka do that; both reveal new aspects of Torah, but Purim is a new text and mitzva that

---

[133] See page 94.

is sourced in Torah - it manifests during the era of prophecy and extends the prophetic mode of Torah. It transgresses no prohibition of addition because its source is already in Torah. Chanuka adds no text to Torah, and although its mitzva is added to Jewish practice, it is a creation of the Oral Law. Just as all the Oral Law is an expression of the wisdom of the Sages, Chanuka is that too. The Oral Law derives Purim from within the Written Law; the Oral Law creates Chanuka of its own legitimate authority.

Chapter 20

Tisha B'Av - Why Mourning Lessens as the Day Progresses

All festivals reveal new Torah. What new Torah is brought to the world by Tisha B'Av, the festival of mourning?

Tisha B'Av commemorates the destruction of the Temple with an intense national mourning. The day requires observing the laws of mourning; however, the laws of mourning are less stringent in the afternoon - from noon, the sadness begins to lift.[134]

But why is the afternoon's sadness less? The fact is that the Temple was set on fire in the afternoon (and it burned through the next day). If anything, the mourning should intensify in the afternoon; that is when the actual destruction took place. This question is asked by Arizal (Kavanot).

---

[134] The halachic requirements are somewhat relaxed from noon - for example, one is no longer required to sit on the floor.

Describing the entry of the destroyers into the Temple, the psalm (Psalms 79) begins: *"Mizmor l'Asaf* - A song of Asaph... strangers have entered your Sanctuary." The Midrash (Eicha Rabba 4; Rashi, Kiddushin 31b) asks:

> "A song of Asaf... strangers have entered your Sanctuary." Why is this called a song [it is describing destruction, not salvation]? It should have stated: "A lamentation of Asaf." [The answer is that] Asaf sang because God vented His anger on the wood and stones of His house and thereby spared the remnant of Israel. Had he not done so there would have remained no remnant of... Israel. As the verse (Eicha 4:11) says: "God expended His anger and ignited a fire in Zion..."

The Midrash is teaching that only because God's anger was expressed in the physical destruction of a building, the Jewish people survived - if not for that destruction, nothing would remain of the Jewish people. What lies behind this idea of God's venting His anger on a building instead of on His people? Why is the destruction of the physical structure of the Temple a reason for saving the people?

The commentary Tosfot (Gittin 2a) states that a *get*, a bill of divorce, is written in twelve lines (the *gematria* of *"get"* is twelve) - since in a Torah scroll there are four lines between each of the books, there are twelve lines of separation in all. (Divorce is a separation of the intense oneness of marriage; the law of its agent, the *get*, derives from the separation between the books of Torah.) But of course there should be sixteen lines - there are four breaks between five books. Tosfot answers that the break between the last two books, Bamidbar and Devarim, is not to be counted because the book of Devarim is "only repetition." What does this mean?

Another question: Jeremiah ends Eicha (Lamentations) on a note of destruction: "You have shown us extreme anger." We traditionally add a line of hope and prayer for redemption when we read the book: "Return us to You and we will return..." (this is in fact the penultimate line; we repeat it in order to end on a positive note). Why do we end with a verse that is not the one Jeremiah chose to end with? Why not stay true to the original text - how can we add a line of hope that Jeremiah could not?

The *gemara* (Yoma 69b) states:

> Rabbi Yehoshua ben Levi said: Why is their title "The Men of the Great Assembly?" Because they returned the crown to its former greatness. Moses came and said: "God who is *gadol, gibor v' nora* - great, mighty and awesome." Jeremiah came and said: "Gentiles are crowing in His Temple; where is His awesomeness?" - he [therefore] omitted "awesome." Daniel came and said: "Gentiles are enslaving His children; where is His might?" - he [therefore] omitted "mighty." They [the Great Assembly] came and said: "On the contrary, that is precisely His great might - that He restrains Himself and allows the wicked to continue; and that is precisely His awesomeness - if not for that awe, how could one nation [Israel] survive among the [murderous] nations?"

The Midrash (Tanchuma, Toldot 5; Esther Rabba 10:11) comments:

> Caesar said to Rabbi Yehoshua: "Great is the sheep that survives among seventy wolves." He replied: "Great is the Shepherd Who saves it and protects it..."

Originally, Moses stated: "God, who is *gadol, gibor v' nora* - great, mighty and awesome." Jeremiah omitted the term *nora* - he was describing the destruction; he could not describe God as awesome when strangers were trampling the courtyards of the Temple in its desecration. The verse (Psalms 68) states: *"Nora Elokim mi'mikdashecha* - God [you are] awesome [in] Your Temple." When that is no longer true we cannot say it - we may praise God only with terms that relate to His current manifestation;[135] when he silently allows His honor to be desecrated He cannot be called awesome.

---

[135] There is a general rule that God should be praised only with a *midda* (trait) that is currently manifest: if one says *"HaMelech haKadosh* - the Holy King" in prayer during the year (when God's kingship is not revealed), that prayer is invalid, and if one fails to say it during the Ten Days of Repentance (when God's kingship is manifest) the prayer is similarly invalid. Every statement that describes Divine conduct must correspond to what is actually revealed of that conduct in the world when the statement is made.

For the same reason, Daniel omitted the term *gibor* - he saw the Jews in Persian exile; he could not describe God as mighty when enemies were enslaving the Jews.

The Great Assembly, however "Returned the crown to its former glory" - they reinstated the term *nora* to our liturgy. "On the contrary, that is His greatness" - He allows desecration of his honor and remains silent; *that* is an awesome mode of conduct. He allows His honor to be cast down; instead of revealing Himself openly by destroying the wicked to uphold His honor, He ensures the survival of the Jewish people in the face of constant genocidal attempts, and that is how we see Him manifest. That is an awesome manifestation: in the indirect display of His power in our survival against impossible odds. His silence is His awesomeness. In place of: "Who is like You among the *eilim* - powerful ones" (Psalms 89b), the Sages read: "Who is like You among the *ilmim* - silent ones" (Gittin 56b).

The mode of God's operation in the world has changed; where it was formerly manifest openly as His glory in the Temple, it has become His covert guaranteeing of the Jewish people's survival despite the constant threat of annihilation. He no longer speaks openly; He has retreated to operate silently from behind the scenes.

But if that is indeed awesome, why could Jeremiah not say so? What gives the Great Assembly the power to express what Jeremiah did not?

The answer is this: during Jeremiah's prophetic era, when God's glory is insulted by trespassers and desecrators in His Temple and He remains silent, He cannot be praised as awesome. The inner precincts of the Temple, so holy that if a stranger enters he should die, is no longer revealing that awesome power. Jeremiah cannot express it because it is not currently true. But when God steps back; when He operates in the world from behind the scenes, sustains us against all odds and gives us the power to create Torah from within a genocidal exile, we can praise Him for that awesome withholding of His might. When He no longer appears openly but gives the Oral Law dominant status, we can once again assert that greatness in the form of an entirely new Torah that lights an intense darkness. That conduct began with the Great Assembly and they pointed to it as His greatness; in their day *that was God's current mode* and He must be praised in terms of the mode of His current operation. When that became the operative mode they could praise Him for it.

From the point of view of prophecy, the tragedy of His hiding Himself is indescribable. Nothing could be worse. But from the point of view of the Oral Law, it is everything: without His hiding there would be no Oral Law, no opportunity for us to reveal His greatness from within ourselves.

In the Temple's destruction the prophet sees the end of revelation, the tragedy of separation, he hears the echoes of a cosmic divorce. But in that same destruction the Sages see the birth of a new paradigm, a dark world in which we will be preserved to become the home for the Divine. The removal of the place of open revelation from the world has become the reason for the Jewish people's survival.

The place where God speaks openly - the place from which the voice of the Written Law can be heard - is destroyed. Now the Torah moves into the hearts and minds of the Jewish people. We contain Torah within us now; we are the Holy Ark. Jeremiah could not end on a positive note: he represents prophecy and he has seen that die. The second to last verse that speaks of hope - "Return us to You and we will return..." - is overridden by the last verse, a verse of destruction. That is precisely what manifests to Jeremiah and that is what he must express.

But we can end on that verse of hope. When the wood and stones of the Temple are destroyed the Torah moves into us. The prophetic mode has disappeared, but that is exactly what opens the mode of the Oral Law; *because the Temple has been destroyed* and the open glory of God is no longer manifest we can express an entirely new Torah. The redemptive element within the destruction is the shift of mode; the incineration of the vessel of the higher mode makes possible a new revelation in a new vessel. Within the tragedy a new light is kindled; in the tragedy that the prophet experiences as his world is extinguished we see a new light dawn. Jeremiah sees the tragedy of God's departure; we see His arrival, indirectly, in the miracle of our survival. Jeremiah could not say *nora*, but the Great Assembly could.

Nora and *Aron*

Ramban (Shmot 25:1) states that the purpose of the Mishkan (Sanctuary; later the Temple) was to be the home of the *aron*.[136] *Nora* is *aron* in reverse (Etz Chaim, Shaar 36; Arizal adds that *aron* in *gematria* is also equal to *nezer,* crown). Our travels through the desert are led by the *aron,* the vessel that holds the Torah. Wherever we travel the *aron* accompanies us. When the *aron* is hidden, we become the *aron;* Torah now travels through history within us.

Our Torah is not the Torah of prophets. Moses could not understand the Torah of Rabbi Akiva (Menachot 29b); a Torah that has to be derived in the context of doubt was not Moses' version of the Torah. We are an entirely new vessel for Torah; awesome in an entirely new way.

New Connection

The book of Devarim continues from the previous four books of Torah without a separation; there may be a gap in the text, but the books are not separated - the lines between books that form the basis of a *get*, a bill of divorce, are not these lines. The book of Devarim is the book of the receiver, the precursor of the Oral Law, and that is bonded to the Written Torah in a unique way. The organic connection between Written and Oral Law is being laid down here - that is connection, not separation; these are not lines that could count towards the separation of divorce.

Afternoon Fire

The Temple burned in the afternoon, a time that moves into night. At that time, when the Temple became a burned out shell, the Holy Ark and its contents shifted to a new home. That is why the mourning begins to lift at this time. When the Torah is banished from its natural home, it begins its march through history in a new home - in the creative hearts and minds of a people miraculously surviving millennia of concentrated hatred. The burning of the physical building has driven its contents into a new Ark, an indestructible portable home that will travel through the "desert of the nations" (Yechezkel 20:35) until it returns, at the end of history, to its original place. Within the Temple's destruction, the seeds of its redemption have been sown.

---

[136] When Jacob dreamed of the ladder and awoke with a start on realising he had been sleeping on the spot that would later become the Temple, he exclaimed: *"Ma nora ha'makom ha'zeh...-* How awesome is this place." *Nora* - awesome; and precisely the letters of *Aron*, the Ark that would later come to rest there.

VI:
Personalities of Transition

Chapter 21

Three Fathers Who Began History - Twice

The Deeds of the Fathers are a Sign for the Children
The two phases of history run parallel, the first in a higher mode and the second in a lower one. This is none other than an expression of *"Ma'aseh avot siman l'banim* - The deeds of the fathers are a sign for the children." Every seminal event in Jewish history is echoed later at a lower level, and in fact the second event is a precedent for yet another parallel event that will occur later still, forming a cascade of refracted events throughout all of history.

Ramban (Genesis 12:6) states:

> I will inform you of a general principle that applies in all the forthcoming sections dealing with Abraham, Isaac and Jacob; it is a major principle mentioned briefly by our Sages. They have said (Tanchuma 9): "All that happened to the Fathers is a sign for the children;" and therefore the verses describe at length the travels, the excavation of wells and other events [that occurred to the Fathers]. One who considers these events may take [the Torah's describing] them to be unnecessary and with no benefit,

but in fact they all come to teach about the future; for any event concerning the three Fathers will indicate to a prophet that it is destined to occur to the children at some point...

Ramban goes on to say that the presaging event experienced by the Fathers is more than simply advance information: rather, each such event brings a reality into the world that ensures that the derivative event will happen later in history. A prophetic prediction may be subject to change under certain conditions; but a prediction accompanied by an action or event solidifies into inevitability.[137]

Parallels: Abraham, Isaac, Jacob and Chananya, Mishael, Azarya

Maharal (Gevurot Hashem 61 and 64) shows how Abraham, Isaac and Jacob were paralleled later by Chananya, Mishael and Azarya - the former three began the first phase of history as the original fathers and the latter three reflect that work as they introduce the second phase. Abraham was thrown into a furnace by Nimrod for his beliefs and survived; Chananya, Mishael and Azarya survived Nevuchadnezzar's furnace in a parallel ordeal. That event occurred on the cusp of the transition between eras: the last three prophets (Chaggai, Zecharia and Malachi) lived at the same time; Chananya, Mishael and Azarya ushered in a new era beyond the reach of prophecy, just as the forefathers had begun the prophetic phase of Jewish history long before.

This parallel goes further. Maharal (Gevurot Hashem 61) explains that when God protects His righteous ones, He does so from one of three specific roots: either from *chessed,* kindness, that is, doing more than strictly required, because His righteous ones act with that quality towards Him; or from *din,* a strict justice because the evil ones who are acting against the righteous deserve that; or from *kavod,* for the sake of His glory. The three qualities of *chessed, din* and *kavod* are precisely the qualities brought to the world by Abraham, Isaac and Jacob respectively. Maharal shows how Chananya, Mishael and Azarya each attribute their salvation to one of these three qualities, and indeed how each of them embodies one of these. Each one's praise is an expression of his essence, just as each of the forefathers' lives expresses the quality that he uniquely builds in the world.

---

[137] See Drashot HaRan (second Drasha) for an extended discussion of this principle as it applies to the Fathers and also to later prophets and prophecies.

Chananya, Mishael and Azarya - each embodies his quality in a manner analogous to the qualities of *chessed, din* and *kavod* brought to the world by the forefathers and each expresses himself in terms of his unique quality - Maharal (Gevurot Hashem 64) shows this in detail: the three expressions in Hallel *"Lo lanu* - Not for our sake," *"L'shimcha ten kavod* - Give honor to Your Name," and *"Al chasdecha* - For your kindness" were said by Chananya, Mishael and Azarya respectively. The first, "Not for our sake," indicates the quality of *din*, perfect justice, because the phrase invokes a conduct of perfection, far above what we could claim in our own right or for our sake. "Give honor to Your Name" explicitly designates the quality of *kavod*, honor. And "For Your kindness" explicitly designates *chessed*, kindness.

The terms *chen, chessed* and *rachamim* (mercy) are expressions of *din, chessed* and *kavod* respectively, as we find in the Grace after meals: "You nourish the world with *chen, chessed v'rachamim*..." (see Maharal there for these parallels and his detailed exposition).

The names Chananya, Mishael and Azarya reflect these qualities. "Chananya" indicates *din:* the root of Chananya, *chen,* indicates something given purely by the decision of the giver, regardless of whether it is deserved (*"chen"* is also the root of *"chinam,"* for free...). This precisely expresses the idea of "Not for our sake," the praise uttered by Chananya. "Mishael" indicates *rachamim,* mercy (parallel to *kavod* as above); the root of Mishael is *"shael,"* to ask, because mercy is given where it is asked for or needed (*chessed* is given purely from the goodness of the giver, *rachamim* is given in response to the receiver's need). "Azarya" indicates *chessed* because the root of Azarya is *azar,* to help - this is the quality that is given by God's right hand, the hand of *chessed.*

Azarya parallels Abraham *(chessed),* Chananya parallels Isaac *(din)* and Mishael parallels Jacob *(kavod).* Just as the world began with these three qualities manifest through the forefathers of the Jewish people, it begins again in its second, post-prophetic phase, with these three latter father figures in parallel fashion.

These are Maharal's words (commenting on the *gemara* in Sanhedrin 92b - there the *gemara* states that God considered destroying the world in blood "but when He looked upon Chananya, Mishael and Azarya, He was appeased"):

"We have already stated that these righteous ones represent distinct qualities (as we have explained in Gevurot Hashem) and that they embodied the qualities of the forefathers who were the foundation of the world. Therefore when God looked upon Chananya, Mishael and Azarya who were [similarly] like the foundation of the world, each of these righteous individuals possessing a unique quality parallel to the three holy Names... and parallel to these, Shimon HaTzaddik stated that the world stands on three things: Torah, service and kindness... therefore when He looked upon Chananya, Mishael and Azarya who represent the three pillars on which the world is built, He was appeased."

Maharal is saying that just as the world was originally built on Abraham, Isaac and Jacob, it was redeemed and rebuilt in analogous fashion on Chananya, Mishael and Azarya. With the departure of the last three prophets from the world,[138] the era that the forefathers introduced ended and a new set of forefathers was required to lay down the foundations of a new world.

"The deeds of the fathers are a sign for the children." History progresses in stepwise fashion, each era paralleling the previous ones in its long march to redemption.

Transitional Personalities - Daniel, Ezra and Nechemia
Maharal explains that Chananya, Mishael, Azarya and Daniel form a unit: the first three correspond to Abraham, Isaac and Jacob, and Daniel corresponds to David - the fourth "leg of the table" (the *midda* or quality of *malchut,* David's *midda*). That fourth aspect ends one complete set and prepares the transition to the next, just as David completes the full array of seven Biblical personalities and is followed by Solomon, the first of a new category.

Daniel, and later Ezra and Nechemia, are the transitional personalities. Joshua's conquest led to the first settlement of the Land; Ezra and Nechemia brought the Jews back to begin the second settlement, which

---

[138] See also Maharal (Sanhedrin 93a) on the parallel between Chananya, Mishael and Azarya, and the last prophets Chaggai, Zecharia and Malachi. See there also for the parallel between these three and three names of Mashiach.

established a *kedusha* (sanctity) that became permanent (the Vilna Gaon points out that the *gematria* of "Joshua" equals that of "Ezra" and "Nechemia"). The books of Daniel and Ezra are part of Scripture, but sections of these books are in Aramaic, a language transitional between Hebrew and other languages. The *gemara* (Sanhedrin 93b) states that Daniel, as a transitional figure, was inferior to the Prophets in one way, but superior in another *(chacham adif mi'navi)*: Chaggai, Zecharia and Malachi[139] were prophets; Daniel was not - but he saw a vision that they did not.

Daniel's mode of understanding was not like that of the prophets: he was required to understand from his own work of perception. On the verse (Daniel 9:2): *"Binoti ba'sefarim* - I understood from the books" the *gemara* (Megilla 12a) comments: "Since [the word] *binoti* is used, it is evident that he erred at first." The faculty of *binah* operates by derivation; in this case by deriving the truth only from grasping the nature of the misunderstanding that leads to it. Daniel understood only after misunderstanding. Unlike a prophet who perceives in a flash of insight, the Sage must understand from a process of reconstruction of mistaken concepts. In this phase of history one can stand only after falling. Any understanding that comes easily with no error that requires correction is probably false.

That is precisely the mode that characterises Talmud Bavli (see above, page 111): definitive conclusions are reached only after imperfect ones are demolished (*hava amina* leads to *maskana* - a tentative, appealing, but wrong construct leads to a superior one). The correct conclusion could not have arisen without the deconstruction of error; that has become part of the truth. It is no accident that this insight into the process of second phase enlightenment is taught in the book of Daniel, the book of transition from prophecy to post-prophetic Rabbinic wisdom.

---

[139] "Malachi was [another name for] Ezra" (Megilla 15a). Malachi was the last prophet; his prophecy ends with the promise of the coming of Mashiach: "Behold, I am sending you Elijah the Prophet before the coming of the great and awesome day of God" (3:23); and he issues the very last instruction that the Jewish people are to receive from the world of prophecy as Torah falls silent and we enter the long night that will precede Mashiach: "Remember the Torah of Moses my servant..."

Abraham and Esther - Parallel Points of Origin

There is another parallel between Abraham and a later figure in Jewish history: Esther. The *gemara* (Megilla 13a) says:

> [The verse (Esther 2:7) states:] "Esther had neither father nor mother." Why then does it go on to say: "When her father and mother had died" [Mordechai took her for a wife]? Rav Acha said: [the repetition indicates that] when her mother became pregnant with her, her father died, and when she gave birth to her, her mother died [so that she did not have a father or mother for even a single day].

Shem MiShmuel (Purim, page 167) commenting on this *gemara* says:

> At that time [Purim] a light was revealed from a secluded and hidden place; that is to say, Mordechai and Esther opened an avenue of access to a very high place that had previously been sealed. [This is why:] the one who redeems must be a person of [total] newness. The nature of a child is to follow the ways of his father and mother, and that is why Esther had neither father nor mother - so that she would be totally a point of origin, as the Midrash (B. Rabba 69) applies the verse "And his Torah he shall study" to Abraham - he had no teacher to instruct him, meaning that he [Abraham] was a point of total originality; (and understand this deeply).

Abraham and Esther have this in common: they both introduced a new phase of history; Abraham for the first time, and Esther for the second. Just as Abraham began his work in the world totally of himself, Esther too, initiated a new pattern. Maharal (Gur Aryeh on Rashi, Genesis 11:32) asks why Abraham abandoned his father Terach in Charan - although the Torah does not document that fact explicitly,[140] it is clear from a calculation of the relevant chronology (see Rashi, Genesis 11:32) that after Abraham left Charan for Canaan at the beginning of his epic life's journey, his father lived on for many years. How could Abraham, the model of kindness and the root of all morality in the world, abandon a

---

[140] To state it explicitly would be a discredit to Abraham; and further, it is not stated explicitly because it is not to be emulated - were it to be stated openly it might suggest an ongoing obligation, and that is certainly not intended. This was a one-time requirement, never to be repeated, as Maharal goes on to explain.

parent? That would seem to go against the most basic of all principles of character refinement; it is clear throughout Torah that honoring parents is one of the most fundamental (and universal) requirements of the ethical life.

Maharal explains that Abraham was a point of origin - and a point of origin, by definition *does not follow anything*. Once (and only once) in history, a beginning was made - the Jewish people were formed by an individual who was not to be a son, but purely a father (*"Avraham"* - the name means "father of a multitude" - Genesis 17:5). Abraham is all newness; he begins a radical departure from all that has gone before, and for this one time in history, he is *required* to abandon his past.[141] He is the one person in history who is not a continuation of his father; the commandment to honor a parent does not apply to him because at the deepest level he is not a son of his father. Terach remains in the old world and Abraham journeys to build the new one.

At that deep level, Abraham has no father. And just as Abraham begins with no parent relevant to his journey and no teacher to show him the way, Esther begins as an orphan, starting with neither father nor mother for even a single day of her life.

---

[141] See Midrash, B. Rabba 39:8 - Abraham was in fact commanded to leave his father. The Torah text however, recounts Terach's death before Abraham's departure - at that level he began his journey as an orphan.

VII:
End of Night

Chapter 22

The Final Dawn

The Third Phase

Two phases - inspiration and revelation followed by their withdrawal so that the work of independent growth can begin. In fact, there is a third phase: it is the result of the first two. When inspiration fires the determination to achieve, and that work is done, the third phase - of reward - is built.

When the inspiration of romance motivates long, loyal years of giving, both harmonise in a third phase of real love. When the inspiration of Egyptian miracles begins the journey through the desert to Sinai, Torah can be received in a cosmic love relationship: the Jews left Egypt in Nissan - the zodiac of that month is the sheep, an animal that follows passively. The next month of Iyar, spent walking through the fierce setting of a desert, is the month of the bull, an animal that expresses its own wilful independence. These are the two opposite modes of first and second phases. The third month, Sivan, is the month of Gemini - twins; when the harmony of all dualities is manifest: the two Tablets, Moses and Aaron, Written and Oral Laws, God and His people.[142]

---

[142] That is the secret of the third: "A three-fold Torah (Torah, Prophets, Writings) [was given] to a three-fold people [Kohanim, Levites, Israelites] by a third-born [Moses] on the third day in the third month" (Shabbat 88a).

The fetus is taught the Torah; it is taken away and must be recaptured through effort, and the result is a third phase of genuine possession of wisdom, acquired by original inspiration and realised by years of work.

The third phase is the unity generated by the harmonising of the first two.

The Final Dawn
To get to that final phase of history, much suffering is experienced and much work is needed. The Messianic era will dawn for a generation that is either fully righteous or wholly lacking (Sanhedrin 98a). If the latter is to be the case, the breakdown must be complete - Maharal writes that if a building is demolished to enable rebuilding, unless the demolition is total the new building cannot be called truly new. As long as two bricks of the old structure remain connected, the new building is at least partly old. If the Messianic world is to be genuinely new, the old world must break down totally.[143]

(A *baal teshuva* - newly observant individual - once asked Rabbi Moshe Shapira this question: If the breakdown of the present order must be so profound that no goodness can remain to allow the Messianic age to dawn, are we not obstructing that process by our religious efforts? It would seem that every mitzva we perform is delaying the redemption...

Rabbi Shapira answered: The designation of this generation as *baalei teshuva* is inaccurate. A *baal teshuva* is a person who was originally fully knowledgeable and observant, who defected from his Torah observance, and later found his way back in repentance and self-correction. This generation's *"baalei teshuva"* are people who never knew their Judaism in the first place. They are not returning sinners; rather, they are people with a sensitivity to a new reality that is awakening in the world. They sense a new dawn breaking and they are responding to it. They have seen the emptiness of their culture and their society and they long for a new world. Their reality is the future one that is stirring and awakening, and they are living in that dimension, in that new world that their consciousness senses, and *their accounts are written on the dawn that is*

---

[143] See Ramchal, Daat Tevunot and other works of his for a definitive approach to this issue. The kabbalistic tradition teaches that all the *gevurot* (harsh and potentially destructive spiritual elements) must be fully expressed in order to be reconstructed in the new order.

breaking, not here at all. Their Torah and good deeds belong to that new world; that is where they are living in essence. Their goodness is not of this world, and they are not hindering the redemption in the least.)

The Last Hope
But if the fact is that this order must grind down to its dismal end, and in the decline of history we are the smallest of all generations, merely the dead skin of the heels of the supernal human form, how can we generate any enthusiasm for our work in the world? How can we expect to achieve anything meaningful? We look at prayer, for example: the Prophets prayed for the Messianic redemption, and quite evidently failed. The gigantic souls of the Mishnaic period tried, and they too were unsuccessful (despite their mighty power of prayer: when Rabbi Akiva merely began *preparing* to pray for rain, the rain fell). But his requests for Mashiach failed. What hope is there for us? When an ordinary Jew prays today, standing among the shreds of our generation's spiritual disintegration, how can he put any sincerity into his prayer - can he really believe that his minuscule effort will bring Mashiach?

The answer to that challenge is this. The decline of history is real; we are almost powerless compared to our great forebears, that is true. But the decline of history is a living continuum; we are part of a living body, and in a complete body the bottom of the feet are necessary too. We are one organic structure; that structure began with Abraham, Isaac and Jacob, and it continues to this day. All that we do joins the long chain of creation that spans history.

Prayer too, is a project of the entire Jewish people, spread over the entirety of history. A barrel of prayer and tears needs to be filled, and it will take all of history to fill it. When the prophets prayed, they poured enormous amounts into that barrel. When the holy personalities of the Mishna prayed, they added gallons. As history progresses each declining generation adds less, *but the barrel is getting fuller.* At the end of history it will be brimming, and some almost hopeless broken-hearted Jew will utter one last faint prayer - and fill the barrel.

Glossary, Biographical Notes and Historical Chart

Glossary and Biographical Notes

Akeidat Yitzchak (Akeida): Torah commentary by R. Isaac ben Moshe Arama; 1420 - 1494 (Spain).

Acharon: "last;" set of Talmudic commentaries from 16th century to the present day

amidah: ("standing" prayer); central part of prayer service

Arizal: R. Isaac ben Shlomo Luria Ashkenazi; 1534 - 1574 (Tzfat), central figure in the kabbalistic tradition.

Avodat HaMelech: R. Menachem Mendel ben Zvi Hirsh Krakowsky; 1870-1930 (Lithuania).

Avot: see Pirkei Avot

aron: ark; the Ark of the Covenant

ba'al teshuva: one who has repented and corrected his ways

bechira: free choice

Bet Din: Jewish court of law

Bet Halevi: R. Yosef Dov Soloveitchik of Brisk; 1820 - 1892.

Chafetz Chaim: R. Yisrael Meir Hacohen Kagan; 1839 (Vilna) –1933 (Radin). Author of Chafetz Chaim, Shemirat HaLashon and Mishne Berura with Bi'ur Halacha and Sha'ar HaTzion, commentary on Shulchan Aruch.

Chazon Ish: R. Avraham Yeshaya Karelitz, 1878 (Kosov, Lithuania) - 1953 (Bnei Brak).

Chashmonaim: the Hasmonean heroes of the Chanuka era

Chaver: R. Yitzchak Isaac Chaver; 1789 - 1852, second generation student of the Vilna Gaon.

Chemdat Shlomo: R. Shlomo Zalman Lipshitz; d. 1839 (Posen).

chessed: kindness; kabbalistically the root quality of unlimited giving; counterpoised to *din*

Chida: R. Chaim Joseph David Azulai; 1724-1806 (Israel and Italy). Author of a commentary on the Shulchan Aruch titled 'Birkei Yosef,' Shem HaGedolim and many other works.

Chinuch: see Sefer HaChinuch

daat: knowledge; deep understanding

Dessler: R. Eliyahu Eliezer Dessler; 1891 - 1954 (Russia, London and Ponovezh Yeshiva in Bnei Brak), author of Michtav M'Eliyahu.

din: strict justice; kabbalistically the root of withholding or restriction, counterpoised to *chessed*

Drashot HaRan: Set of essays *(drashot)* on fundamental Torah themes by Ran (see Ran).

Eidels: R. Samuel Eliezer Eidels (Maharsha), 1555 - 1632 (Cracow). Known primarily for his commentary on the Talmud.

Emden: R. Jacob ben Tzvi Emden (Yaavetz), 1697 - 1776 (Altona). Son of the Chacham Zvi. Authored works on Mishnah, Talmud, kabbala, the prayer book and responsa, *Yaarot Devash, She'elat Yavetz* and *Mor u'K'tzia* on Orach Chaim.

Gaon of Vilna: (*gaon:* lit. "genius") R. Eliyahu ben Shlomo Zalman of Vilna; 1720–1797.

gemara: Talmud, the Oral Law; more specifically the analysis and discussion of the Mishna.

Gevurot Hashem: Work by Maharal; Rabbi Yehuda Loewe ben Bezalel of Prague, c.1512 - 1609.

Gur Aryeh: Torah commentary by Maharal; Rabbi Yehuda Loewe ben Bezalel of Prague, c.1512 - 1609.

HaChassid: R. Yehuda HaChassid, b. ca.1150 (Speyer, Germany) - 1217 (Regensburg). Author of Sefer Chassidim.

halacha: Torah law

Hashem: lit. "the Name" of God

Hutner: R. Yitzchak Hutner; 1906 (Warsaw) - 1980 (Jerusalem). Author of Pachad Yitzchak.

Izhbitzer: R. Mordechai Yosef Leiner of Izhbitz; 1801-1854 (Tomashov, Izhbitz). Hasidic thinker and founder of the Izhbitz-Radzyn dynasty. Student of R. Simcha Bunim of Pshischa and R. Menachem Mendel of Kotzk. Author of Mei HaShiloach. Rabbi of R. Zaddok HaCohen.

kabbala: esoteric Torah wisdom

Kamenetsky: R. Yaakov Kamenetsky; 1891 – 1986 (Lithuania, USA).

keruvim: angels; the angelic forms on the cover of the *aron*

Kli Yakar: work by R. Shlomo Ephraim ben Aaron Luntschitz; 1550 - 1619, (Luntschitz).

Kotler: R. Aharon Kotler; 1891 – 1962 (Lithuania, New York). Founded Lakewood Yeshiva, New Jersey.

Kovetz Shiurim: Work by R. Elchanan Wasserman.

Leshem Shvo V'Achlama: Works by R. Shlomo Elyashiv (also known as Leshem or Ba'al HaLeshem); 1841 - 1926, (Lithuania, Jerusalem). Grandfather of R. Yosef Shalom Elyashiv.

Luzzatto: R. Moshe Chaim Luzzatto (Ramchal); 1707 - 1746 (Padua, Venice, Amsterdam), author of The Path of the Just (Mesillat Yesharim) classic *mussar* work and many other works.

Maharal of Prague: R. Yehuda Loewe ben Bezalel, ca.1512 - 1609.

Maharsha: see Eidels.

Malbim: R. Meir Leibush ben Yechiel Michel Wisser; 1809 - 1879, (Bucharest, Königsberg).

Maimonides: R. Moshe ben Maimon (Rambam), 1135 (Cordova) - 1204 Egypt. Authored Mishneh Torah (also known as Yad HaChazakah), Guide to the Perplexed, hundreds of responsa and numerous medical works.

malchut: "kingship;" tenth and final of the Divine emanations

mazal, mazalot: zodiac element(s)

megilla: scroll; such as the Megilla of Esther

midda: Divine, or character, trait

Midrash: Torah sources which delve deeper than the plain meaning of the Scriptural text.

Minchat Chinuch: R. Yosef ben Moshe Babad 1801 (Tarnopol) - 1874 (Tzfat). His Minchat Chinuch is a collection of essays on the 613 mitzvot through the perspective of the Talmud and Rishonim, structured as a commentary on the Sefer HaChinuch.

Mishna: the definitive statements of the Oral Law, codified in their present form by Rabbi Judah the Prince (approx. 2nd century C.E.).

mitzva; mitzvot: commandment(s)

Moreh HaNevuchim: Guide to the Perplexed by Rambam

mussar: the study and practice of Torah character building

Nachmanides: R. Moshe ben Nachman (Ramban), 1194 (Gerona) - 1270 (Israel). Authored commentaries on the Bible and Talmud, halachic codes, responsa, works on mysticism and philosophy.

Nefesh HaChaim: work by R. Chaim (Ickovitz) of Volozhin; disciple of Vilna Gaon, 1749 - 1821.

neshama: soul

Noda B'Yehuda: Work by R. Yechezkel ben Yehuda Landau, 1713 (Poland) - 1793 (Prague). Also authored Dagul Mervavah on Shulchan Aruch and Tziyun l'Nefesh Chayah (Tz'lach).

Ohr HaChaim: Torah commentary by R. Chaim ben Moshe ibn Attar; 1696 (Morocco) - 1743 (Jerusalem). Teacher of Chida.

Ohr Somayach: R. Meir Simcha HaKohen; 1843 (Vilna, Bialystok) - 1926 (Dvinsk). Authored a commentary on Rambam, and Meshech Chochmah on Chumash.

Pirkei Avot: Ethics of the Fathers; section of Mishna dealing mainly with ethical teachings.

Ralbag: R. Levi ben Gershon Catalan (Gersonides); 1288 - 1344 (France).

Rambam: see Maimonides

Ramban: see Nachmanides

Ramchal: see Luzzatto

Ran: R. Nissim ben Reuben Gerondi; 1315 - 1375 (Gerona).

Rashi: R. Shlomo Yitzchaki (R. Shlomo ben Yitzchak), 1040 - 1105 (Troyes). Pre-eminent commentator on Torah and Talmud.

ratzon: desire, will, volition

Rishon: "first;" set of Talmudic commentaries from 10th to 15th centuries.

Rosh: R. Asher ben Yechiel, 1250 (Germany) - 1327 (Toledo). Authored commentary on the Talmud and more than 1,000 responsa. Father of the Tur.

Rozovsky: R. Shmuel Rozovsky; 1913 (Grodno) - 1979 (Bnei Brak). Student of R. Shimon Shkop.

ruach ha'kodesh: Divine inspiration

Saadia: R. Saadia Gaon (Saadia ben Joseph); 882/892 (Egypt) - 942 (Baghdad), prominent teacher and philosopher of the Geonic period. Author of Emunot V'Deot.

Sefer Chassidim: see HaChassid

Sefer HaChinuch: Published anonymously in 13th century Spain. Systematically discusses the 613 commandments of the Torah.

sefirot: Divine emanations

Seridei Eish: R. Yechiel Yaacov Weinberg; 1885 - 1959 (Germany and Switzerland).

Shechina: the Divine Presence

Shem MiShmuel: R. Shmuel Bornshtain; 1855 - 1926 (Sochatchov). Second Rebbe of the Sochatchov dynasty. Known as the Shem Mishmuel by the title of his work on Torah and Chassidic thought.

Sforno: R. Ovadiah ben Jacob Sforno; c.1475 (Cesena) - 1550 (Bologna).

Shibbolei HaLeket: R. Tzidkiyah HaRofei Anav; 1230 - 1300 (Italy).

shmoneh esreh: "eighteen" part central prayer of the daily prayer service

Soloveitchik: R. Chaim haLevi Soloveitchik; 1853 (Volozhin) - 1918 (Otwock, near Warsaw). Introduced a particular analytical methodology to Talmudic study.

Talmud: the Oral Law; comprising Mishna and *gemara*

tefilla: prayer

tikkun: correction

Torah: the Five Books of Moses; or more generally all of Scripture, the Oral Law and commentaries.

Tosfot: Set of classic commentaries on the Talmud composed during twelfth to fourteenth centuries, printed in all standard editions of the Babylonian Talmud. Included Rashi's grandson R. Yaacov ben Meir Tam (Rabbenu Tam), and Rashi's nephew R. Isaac ben Shmuel (Ri).

tzaddik, tzaddikim: righteous individual(s)

tzelem: image

urim v'tumim: elements of the High Priest's breastplate; they would cause it to reveal prophetic information

Volozhin: R. Chaim Volozhin (Volozhiner); 1749 - 1821 (Volozhin). Leading disciple of the Vilna Gaon. Founded the Volozhin yeshiva ("the mother of all Lithuanian-style yeshivot") in 1803. Author of Nefesh HaChaim.

Wasserman: R. Elchanan Wasserman; Rosh Yeshiva and Torah leader, 1875 (Baranowitch) - martyred 1941 (Kovno). Leading disciple of the Chafetz Chaim. Authored Talmudic commentary and essays.

Wasserman: R. Simcha Wasserman; Rosh Yeshiva and Torah teacher, 1900 - 1992 (Baranowitch, Los Angeles, Jerusalem). Son of R. Elchanan Wasserman.

Yaavetz (She'elat Yaavetz): See Emden.

Yerushalmi: Jerusalem Talmud

Zadok HaCohen: R. Zadok HaCohen Rabinowitz; 1823 - 1900 (Lublin). Student of the Izhbitzer. Author of Tzidkat HaTzaddik, Pri Tzaddik, Takkanat HaShavim, Resisei Layla, Machashavot Charutz, Sichat Malachei HaShareit and other works.

Zohar: foundational kabbalistic work by Mishnaic Sage R. Shimon bar Yochai.

Zonnenfeld: R. Yosef Chaim Zonnenfeld; 1848 - 1932 (Jerusalem).